Early praise for *Build an Awesome PC, 2014 Edition*

I only wish I'd had a guide like this when I got into PC building.

➤ **Henry Thomas**
Former console peasant

Full of pictures and meticulous attention to detail, this book spells out how you can build your dream computer with top-of-the-line components but within a sane budget. Highly recommended!

➤ **Glenn Ferrell, PMP**
President, gfWEBsoft LLC

This is a really great "construction manual" for an awesome PC that anyone can build. For over 40 years people have been building their own computers. Mike's book makes it so easy! You'll be proud of the computer you create.

➤ **Mike Bengtson**
Generalist

Straightforward, informative, and awesome!

➤ **Corey Butler**
Founder, Ecor Ventures

It has been years since I built my own PC. After reading Mike's book, I now want to build an awesome PC with my kids!

➤ **Sven Davies**
IT director, Connect Hearing

An informative, solid, no-nonsense DIY guide to building your own PC, with lots of neat unexpected tips. I got a really good handle on the basics of hardware. I feel confident and enticed now to build my own PC, as the author has made it sound so easy and exciting, with lots of room for technical growth!

➤ **Cristina Zamora**
Software developer

To someone who has built custom computers for over 30 years, this book stands out at a must-have reference for newbies and experienced builders alike. No detail is left out, and you are sure to have a guided and fun experience on your next custom build.

➤ **Jon Kurz**
President, Dycet Research Group

It will be helpful to the first-time builder and even the every-now-and-then builder who needs a "checklist."

➤ **Jeff Horn**
President, Aged Woods, Inc.

This book invokes the "maker spirit" and made me excited to build my own awesome PC. With its step-by-step instructions and illustrations, I felt like the author was there with me as I started my awesome PC endeavor!

➤ **Eric Bruno**
President, Allure Technology, Inc.

This is a wonderful and enjoyable guide to PC assembly; it's clear and gets straight to the point. I definitely recommend this surprisingly light read to anyone building their first high-end gaming machine.

➤ **Ankoor Shah**
   Computer-science major

Mike Riley distills the complex topic of PC building into a concise and easy instruction manual.

➤ **John Cairns**
   Senior engineer, Chicago Trading Company

Build an Awesome PC, 2014 Edition

Easy Steps to Construct the Machine You Need

Mike Riley

The Pragmatic Bookshelf

Dallas, Texas • Raleigh, North Carolina

Many of the designations used by manufacturers and sellers to distinguish their products are claimed as trademarks. Where those designations appear in this book, and The Pragmatic Programmers, LLC was aware of a trademark claim, the designations have been printed in initial capital letters or in all capitals. The Pragmatic Starter Kit, The Pragmatic Programmer, Pragmatic Programming, Pragmatic Bookshelf, PragProg and the linking *g* device are trademarks of The Pragmatic Programmers, LLC.

Every precaution was taken in the preparation of this book. However, the publisher assumes no responsibility for errors or omissions, or for damages that may result from the use of information (including program listings) contained herein.

Our Pragmatic courses, workshops, and other products can help you and your team create better software and have more fun. For more information, as well as the latest Pragmatic titles, please visit us at *http://pragprog.com*.

The team that produced this book includes:

Jacquelyn Carter (editor)
Candace Cunningham (copyeditor)
David J Kelly (typesetter)
Janet Furlow (producer)
Ellie Callahan (support)

For international rights, please contact *rights@pragprog.com*.

Printed in the United States of America.
ISBN-13: 978-1-941222-17-1
Printed on acid-free paper.
Book version: P1.0—May 2014

This book is dedicated to my brother Frank,
who a long time ago in a galaxy known as the
Milky Way introduced me to science fiction,
CP/M, and DOS.

Contents

Acknowledgments

Writing a book is hard work, even when the subject being written about is so much fun. In addition to distilling the critical essence of the topic into effective sentences and paragraphs, there remains a long list of tasks that need to be done before a book is ready for its readership. Without the assistance of skilled editors, artisans, and technical reviewers, this book could have remained on my bucket list until said bucket was kicked.

Fortunately, I got by with plenty of help from my friends. I first wish to thank Jackie Carter, the book's development editor. We've had a wonderfully productive working relationship since my first book for Pragmatic, and I look forward to many more books with her keeping me focused and cheering for me at the finish line.

Many thanks also to my friends who reviewed the technical aspects and helped to greatly clarify the instruction in the book. Henry Thomas assisted even before I typed the first sentence, validating my choice of hardware to promote in the book. He was also there after the last sentence was entered, reminding me to highlight and enhance certain portions. May you build long and prosper, sir. The other people who helped shape and refine this book with their *awesome* comments and suggestions include Cristina Zamora, Eric Bruno, Corey Butler, Mike Bengtson, Glenn Ferrell, John Cairns, Jeff Horn, Sven Davies, Jon Kurz, and Ankoor Shah. This book has surpassed my own high-bar expectations as a result of their insightful and ever-helpful comments and recommendations. And thanks to David Kelly and all the other designers, copy editors, and production folks at The Pragmatic Bookshelf for polishing this book into a gem.

Thanks to my artistically gifted daughter Marielle for rendering the image you see on the computer monitor shown on the cover. Thanks also to my son Mitchell for giving an enthusiastic thumbs-up after stress-testing the final PC build with his selection of the most cutting-edge and graphically demanding games today. And thanks to my wife Marinette for allowing me to turn the awesome PC audio up to eleven (for testing purposes, I swear) and once again allowing me to trade family time for book-writing time.

Finally, I'd like to say a very special thank-you to the Pragmatic Bookshelf publishers, Dave Thomas and Andy Hunt. Your endless enthusiasm, passion for technology, and tireless assistance helping authors to spread their invaluable knowledge keep me energized and eager to learn. Thanks to you, I'm learning from the best.

Preface

Welcome, and thank you for spending your time and resources to learn about building your own x86-based personal computer. This is my first exPress title from The Pragmatic Bookshelf and, as "exPress" implies, I promise to keep things moving along at a fast clip with a minimum of stops along the way. Each chapter will feature a brief introduction to the importance of the parts highlighted and then get right down to work.

While the book is designed as a guide to walk you through each step of the process, the ideal approach would be to read the book first to get an overall understanding of the task at hand. Then when you have the parts and are ready to assemble them, read along for a refresher.

But before we start building our awesome PC, let's take a very brief look back to understand how we got here in the first place.

The Rise, Fall, and Rise of the Personal Computer

When the IBM PC was released in the early '80s, I had an Atari 400 computer and detested it. Not only did it have a horrid membrane keyboard, but it also had a locked-in design. Fortunately, the first IBM personal computer was released shortly afterward. In addition to having an Intel-based chip architecture, the PC design allowed for expansion boards that could swap in better graphics cards, more memory, and better storage. All this could be done without having to resort to replacing the entire computer.

As personal computers became more prevalent in the late 1980s and early 1990s, the PC expanded beyond word processing and electronic spreadsheets. The PC gaming market exploded, driven by rapidly improving hardware and people's expectations for more realistic-looking entertainment scenarios. Better video and audio hardware allowed developers and graphic artists to push the limits of the new medium. This, in turn, pushed the PC-hardware and -accessories manufacturers to even greater technical heights.

But then something happened. Gaming consoles from Microsoft and Sony exceeded the audiovisual fidelity of the PC. Connecting to the Internet from the PC became more interesting than pushing pixels. Then smartphones and tablets made the general consumer PC even less interesting by giving users instant access to the Internet without boot time or security-risk overhead. Microsoft and Sony continued to iterate on their proprietary gaming platforms, further challenging the need for high-end PCs.

And then another thing happened. The proprietary gaming platforms reverted to x86-based architecture. (Microsoft's Xbox One and Sony's PlayStation4 are essentially small-footprint PCs optimized for gaming.) The rise of Valve's Steam service has provided a whole new generation of PC-game developers the chance to become overnight millionaires.[1] The advent of Bitcoin mining has employed the operation of high-end graphics cards to perform the work.[2] Most of all, a growing desire among those with a need to express themselves has exponentially expanded what mass-consumer generic computer companies think a PC should look like and be capable of calculating.

A new generation of digital natives are coming of age in our computing society. They want to show off their individualism and mastery of computing capability. They appreciate the ability to configure their PCs the way they want them to look and perform. They want to get under the hood of their desktop computer case and customize the internals to show off to their friends. The more bling, blinking lights, and shiny components to put on display, the better. Just with like the hot-rod car modifications from the 1950s and '60s, we are experiencing a resurgence of customized-computing expressiveness.

The PC is the ultimate dream car for the digital highway, capable of being assembled exactly the way we want it. And in this book, the PC we will build will drive really, really fast along that binary road.

About This Book

Here's a very brief rundown of the chapters in the book.

In Chapter 1 we establish the ground rules for assembling our computer and get a sneak peek at what the PC will look like once we are finished building it.

In Chapter 2 we select the computer case and power-supply unit (PSU) capable of containing and powering our computer.

---

1. http://store.steampowered.com
2. https://bitcoin.org

In Chapter 3 we look at the central processing unit (CPU), the brain of the PC. Since we need to plug that brain into the rest of the PC's nervous system, we need a motherboard (MOBO for short) that matches the brain's size and computing capacity.

In Chapter 4 we examine and install the short-term and long-term memory where the CPU can store its calculations. Short-term memory used while the computer is running is stored in random-access memory (RAM), and long-term memory is where the results of calculations are stored on magnetic, optical, or solid-state drives for later retrieval (even after the power is turned off).

In Chapter 5 we listen for sound and look at video in the form of premium sound and video peripherals.

In Chapter 6 we connect a display, keyboard, and mouse to our PC. We will also take a look at some additional accessories that will give us an edge at playing certain types of games or stringing together multiple keystrokes with a single keypress.

Lastly, in Chapter 7 we will install software that will make our hardware function as a cohesive unit. While PCs used to equate with Microsoft Windows, we will take a look at alternative operating systems in the form of purpose-built Linux distributions.

The book also has three appendixes. The first one takes a look at advanced topics such as overclocking and water cooling and provides recommendations and tips for taking your PC to the next level. The second appendix contains the complete list of parts used to build our awesome PC. The final appendix lists some useful locations on the Web to visit for more information.

Online Resources

Even though this book provides regimented step-by-step instructions for assembling a high-end personal computer, everyone's experience is different. It's these variations that make for good discussions. There will no doubt be a healthy debate about the choices of hardware I recommend. I welcome you to voice your stories, opinions, questions, and insights on the book's forum page on the Pragmatic Bookshelf website.[3]

You can also contact me directly via my email account, mike@mikeriley.com, or on Twitter: @mriley.

---

3. http://pragprog.com/book/mrpc

Safety First

Computer parts can be expensive. And electricity can be dangerous. While I have done my best to alert you to these facts throughout the book, please read the following disclaimer so you are aware of the risks associated with assembling any kind of electrical components.

Proceed at Your Own Risk. You Have Been Warned!

Your safety is your own responsibility. Use of the instructions and suggestions in this book is entirely at your own risk. The author and The Pragmatic Programmers, LLC, disclaim all responsibility and liability for any resulting damage, injury, or expense as a result of your use or misuse of this information.

It is your responsibility to make sure your activities comply with all applicable laws, regulations, and licenses. The laws and limitations imposed by manufacturers and content owners are constantly changing, as are products and technology. As a result, some of the projects detailed here may not work as described or may be inconsistent with current laws, regulations, licenses, or user agreements, and they may even damage or adversely affect equipment or other property.

Power tools, electricity, and other resources recommended in this book are dangerous unless used properly and with adequate precautions, including proper safety gear. (Note that not all photos or descriptions depict proper safety precautions, equipment, or methods of use.) You need to know how to use such tools correctly and safely. It is your responsibility to determine whether you have adequate skill and experience to attempt any of the assemblies described or suggested here.

Before proceeding, make sure you are comfortable with any risks associated with building a PC. For example, if the idea of dealing with high voltage or sensitive computer parts worries you, then don't do the build yourself. Seek out the assistance of a professional instead. Build this PC only if you agree that you do so at your own risk.

I hope you enjoy building your own PC as much as I have enjoyed writing about assembling one. I look forward to hearing from you about your experiences and seeing photos of your successful PC constructions. See you online!

Mike Riley
mike@mikeriley.com
Naperville, IL, May 2014

CHAPTER 1

Introduction

Before we start purchasing parts and assembling components, we need to establish a few tenets of effective PC construction. We will also fast-forward to the completed assembly to help visualize what we are building. Finally, we will be reminded of the cautionary aspects of building a PC ourselves and how to mitigate those risks as best we can. But let's begin with exploring why building a PC is better than simply buying a prebuilt PC from a vendor.

The Joys of Building Your Own PC

Besides the obvious benefits of knowing exactly what hardware makes your computer run, there are a number of advantages to building your own PC. Building a PC can be an immensely educationally rewarding experience. Parents can also use the opportunity to have their children participate in the assembly process, making a lifelong memory they will be pleasantly reminded of each time they use the computer.

You will also be surprised at how much money you will save building your own PC. Depending on how far up the performance curve you want to push the parts, you can save anywhere from a couple hundred to a couple thousand dollars. The money you save can be put toward even higher-end components that will make your PC even faster!

PC builders also gain confidence in helping family and friends build their own computers, earning further technical recognition while saving a good deal of money in the process. Custom-built PCs also have a much longer lifetime because many of the components can be easily upgraded as hardware improves.

Most of all, building your own PC is just downright fun! The adrenaline rush of anticipation when you first power up the hardware you assembled is magical. And unlike completing a puzzle, a painting, or a model that remains static once constructed, the PC provides years of dynamic entertainment, exploration, education, and excitement.

The Joys of Using Your Own PC

Building a PC is like building a home. Once you're done with construction, you get to settle into your new surroundings. Indeed, the whole reason you build a PC is so that you can use it to do the things you couldn't do without it.

For example, software developers will be able to boot into the operating system (OS) at lightning speed, zip around their development environment, and compile and test their software faster than ever before. Video enthusiasts will be able to use sophisticated nonlinear editors to scrub through raw video faster than ever before. And gamers will be able to run the very latest cutting-edge games at their highest audiovisual settings. Doing so will exceed the graphics capabilities of the latest game consoles and provide the best gaming experience compared to any other computing platform.

Choices, Choices, Choices

The blessing and curse of PC hardware is the fact that it is modular. Each major component can be swapped out with offerings from a variety of manufacturers. As a result, choosing the right part for the job can require a considerable investment in time to competently learn the jargon associated with that part and the believable benefits that each manufacturer has to offer. For example, in the power-supply category, manufacturer Corsair offers eight different classifications, with several products within each. Multiply this by the dozens of other PC power-supply companies, and deciding which one to buy for your computer can be downright paralyzing. The same thing holds true for CPUs, RAM, graphics cards, MOBOs, and other components—it takes years to become a master in each category.

Fortunately, this book will cut through the bewildering assortment of parts by specifically identifying which manufacturer and product model will build an awesome PC for 2014 and beyond. It won't be a bleeding-edge PC, but one that optimizes the cost-versus-performance curve to deliver a machine for less than $2,000. It will also have enough future-proofing to keep it on the leading edge for years to come.

Establishing the Ground Rules

Before we begin with the acquisition of parts and construction of our PC, I need to share a few thoughts on my approach. First and foremost, this book won't compare the variety of hardware components against one another. Not only are there hundreds of websites that do this kind of thing far more exhaustively than I could, but doing so would also dilute the book's primary intention.

You are reading this book because you want to build an awesome PC, not be constantly wondering whether your choice of hardware will be as good as or better than my recommendations. The manufacturers and products I use in this book reflect my personal view and many years of experience building my own personal computers.

I decided to focus on just one component for each category rather than provide a range of choices. If I had included a buffet of parts to choose from, it would have introduced a significant degree of variability in the build. For example, only certain motherboards work with AMD processors, and certain Intel CPUs work only with certain socket sizes. A mix of parts for each category also would have required a potentially confusing matrix comparison for every component suggested. Besides, for those readers who prefer the matrix analysis of price versus performance, there are a number of excellent websites for mixing and matching components for different power-versus-price scenarios. A few of these sites are listed in Appendix 3, *Additional Resources*, on page 99.

I intend to follow up this book with a new edition when necessary to reflect the rapid changes in the still–rapidly evolving PC-hardware space. But the purpose of the book will be constant, which is to provide you with the best parts recommendations and instructions to give you the confidence to assemble your own cutting-edge computer.

What We Will Build

To give you a clear vision of what we will be assembling through the course of this book, Figure 1, *Inside a completely assembled awesome PC*, on page 4 provides a look at the final result.

If you have never built a PC or even opened up a PC case before, this can look a bit intimidating. Fortunately, it's not scary at all once you start learning what each of component is called and understanding the function it serves. Here is a general description of the parts that you see assembled in the photo.

Figure 1—Inside a completely assembled awesome PC

1. Motherboard
2. CPU fan
3. Memory modules
4. DVD-ROM drive
5. PC case
6. Graphics card
7. Solid-state drive
8. Power supply
9. Hard drive

For the complete list of parts required to assemble the awesome PC constructed in this book, review Appendix 2, *The Complete Parts List*, on page 95. There you will find the part, description, and estimated price for the products. You can use this parts list to obtain the items you will need to construct your own awesome PC.

Throughout this book, you will learn what all of these parts do, why they were selected, and how to properly and safely install them. Whenever a step requires additional attention or a cautionary reminder, a special icon will call that out.

The Caution Indicator

 There are several times throughout the build of a new PC that you need to be extra cautious with the assembly. When you see this caution indicator, be alert and follow the instructions with care.

In addition to minimizing the persistent threat of static shock (more on this in the next section), there's the issue of finger oils and improper alignment and/or mounting to be concerned with. So when you see the caution indicator next to a passage in the book, slowly proceed with clean, static-free hands.

Finally, before assembling any parts, verify the inventory inside each package to account for all the screws, brackets, clips, and accessories that are listed in the product's instruction sheet or manual. Nothing ruins a day more than having a build nearly complete only to discover that a part required for an important connection is missing.

Prepare Your Build Area

 A clean, well-lit work area will help you keep track of the parts and tools you need to build your PC.

Before you start building anything, find a low-clutter location with good lighting where you can safely lay out parts and cables. Throughout the course of the PC's assembly, you will be dealing with lots of small cables, clips, and screws. Keeping track of these pieces is paramount, so make sure you have plenty of work space available.

The most important precaution is to build the PC in a static-free environment. That means a room with no carpeting on the floor, as carpet can build up a static charge. Ground yourself before touching any component. You can do this by wearing an antistatic wrist strap while assembling the PC.[1] A single static shock can ruin your PC in an instant, so save your sanity and take the proper precautions!

Get Ready, Get Set...

With our static-free build area clean and ready to go, we're about to embark on our journey. Here are just a few more quick tips to keep in mind as you assemble the computer.

---

1.   http://en.wikipedia.org/wiki/Antistatic_wrist_strap

- If this is the first time you have built a PC, avoid the use of electric screwdrivers. While manual screw drivers may require slightly more strength and time, they also provide finesse and a feel for the proper threading and tension of the delicate screws used in most PC assemblies.

- Parts should fit firmly together, but not forcefully. If something isn't sliding in or seating properly, check for any obstructions in the connecting areas. Also verify that the parts are in the correct orientation.

- Many of the steps in this book can be done in a different order, but try your best to follow along if this is your first PC assembly. It's easier and far more predictable to follow a well-worn path than try to make your own on the fly.

- Most of all, have fun building your PC. While the reward of using your custom-built PC is the goal, the journey is the most memorable part.

After you overcome your initial trepidation of assembling expensive hardware without harming it or yourself, you can venture further into the hardware-analysis zone that experienced PC builders eventually arrive at. That is because you will have a PC built with modular parts that can be easily swapped out and modified to best suit your changing needs.

In the next chapter we're going to start assembling our PC with a great-looking, functional PC case and a top-quality power supply. Go!

CHAPTER 2

Case and Power Supply

Some PC builders might prefer to begin their construction with the CPU and motherboard. I recommend starting with the case and power supply. The case is indicative of your intent for the hardware it will contain. The type of case you use also makes a statement to the world regarding your high-tech aesthetics.

Since we are going to build a high-end PC drawing upon plenty of electricity and generating a considerable amount of heat, we need a chassis large enough to circulate enough air to cool down a blazingly fast CPU and a beefy graphics card. We also need a power supply that can safely deliver all the conditioned electrical current we need to drive these power-hungry parts.

If this is the first PC you have built, it's also a good idea to buy a case that has plenty of room for your components, plus room to maneuver. It can be extremely frustrating to discover that the beautiful case you acquired is a few centimeters too small to house your graphics card, or that the CPU-cooling fans rise too high above the motherboard to allow the case to close. Let's begin with selecting a case for our awesome PC.

Selecting a Case That Suits You

PC cases come in nearly limitless shapes, sizes, colors, and materials. Some are made of plastic, a few (mostly homebrew) use wood, but most are made of a metal frame and a colored and occasionally textured polyurethane exterior. But the one thing they all have in common is their intent to house a motherboard and accompanying parts. The case shields these electronics from the dangers of dust buildup and static electricity. Some of the best cases also aid with shaping and maximizing the movement of air through the chassis to efficiently cool down hot CPUs and graphics processing units

(GPUs). And of course there's the personal opinion of what looks attractive. Let's take a closer look at these attributes to help us choose an ideal case.

PC-Parts Container

When choosing a case, the most important consideration is the types of components it will house. Our PC will contain a powerful CPU, a decked-out motherboard, and a huge graphics card, along with sticks of RAM, two hard drives, a sound card, and possibly a few other internal peripheral add-ons. While we could attempt to shove all that hardware into a small box, doing so would be painful. It would also concentrate heat buildup to levels harmful to the expensive components we will be installing.

A large case will make it much easier to install, work on, and swap out components. But its bulky size will also make it less than ideal for lugging to LAN parties or using in other portable scenarios. If this is your first time building a PC, give yourself the space and airflow to afford getting acquainted with the process.

Case Airflow

Besides being zapped by static electricity, the other environmental killer of expensive computer parts is heat. With the billions of transistors on CPUs and GPUs, along with the variety of other sensitive electronic parts on the motherboard, heat builds up rapidly once the power starts flowing. The first sign of heat stroke is typically random lock-ups and weird visual glitches. If fans are working and temperature controlled, they will be operating at their maximum revolutions per minute (RPM). The smaller the fan, the louder it will sound. If the system doesn't cool down, permanent component damage could result.

To combat the effects of heat buildup, you need a case that will provide ample space for air to move along an escape route. So in addition to a large open area inside the case, you want a case with plenty of fans or areas to mount fans. The fans should be positioned so they maximize the outflow of hot air from the case. However, having too many fans can make the computer unbearably loud, even when it is idle, with a static image on screen. Some motherboards come with software that can regulate the fans based on internal case temperature.

If silence is the most important factor, you can opt for the more expensive and far more elaborate use of water cooling coupled with an external radiator. But that's an advanced topic that requires a bit more skill and financial resources than traditional air cooling. So for now our computer will be air cooled via conventional fans fitted onto the case.

The Importance of Look and Feel

Cases vary widely in design due to the broad spectrum of individual tastes. Some cases can be massive like a stretch limousine, while others can be small like a subcompact car. Some draw attention to themselves with fins, flashing lights, and bright colors like a sports car while others are reserved and business-formal like a luxury car.

Keeping in mind airflow and the number of components you will be placing into the case, find a case that you consider attractive. Bigger cases usually equate to bigger price tags. Types of materials used can also drive up the cost. An all-aluminum chassis or one using a wood like mahogany will be quite a bit more expensive than a traditional metal frame with a plastic exterior.

Given all these considerations, I recommend going with Corsair's Carbide Series 500R mid tower.[1] It's large enough to comfortably fit our PC components and has enough fans to keep the air circulating. The 500R will also provide adequate room for additional fans should we need them. The fan mounts can even support water-cooling radiators when you're ready to take the hardware into the realm of serious heat-generating overclocking. There are also plenty of relocatable cages for disk-based hard drives and solid-state drives for both present and future storage needs.

Once you have the case, find a place to unpack it and inventory the contents. Be sure to do this in a spot with plenty of open space. When removing the 500R case from the box, use the plastic bag wrapped around it to lift it up. Set the bagged case down gently, as the metal can dent easily. Then remove the bag, being careful not to scratch the painted metal sides.

Inspect the case for any damage. Unscrew and remove the side of the case that has the large fan attached to it. Place the freestanding side somewhere safe, such as against a wall or back in the case's shipping box between the Styrofoam packaging pieces. Did I mention to handle the case with care? If you dent the metal, you will be reminded about that accident every time you look at your case. Gently spin the case fans located on the front, back, and side panel with your finger to verify that they turn without obstruction. A white box of parts should be located in the lower-right drive bin. Check the packing list on the case's instruction sheet to verify that all the parts are included, as Figure 2, *All parts present and accounted for*, on page 10 shows.

With our case picked out, let's take a look at the attributes that make up a good PC power supply.

---

1.   http://www.corsair.com/us/pc-cases/carbide-series-pc-case/carbide-series-500r-white-mid-tower-case.html

Figure 2—All parts present and accounted for

Selecting a Power Supply That Suits Your Hardware

An awesome PC needs an awesome power-supply unit (PSU) to deliver the juice to some seriously power-hungry hardware. Because we are going to be using a fast processor and an even faster graphics card, we need a power supply that can handle the load that this computing hardware will demand. And because a good power supply is a relatively expensive investment, we need our purchase to cover future electricity demands.

For example, when you're ready to pair two or more powerful graphics cards for even greater graphic resolution and performance, your power requirements will elevate considerably. If you initially install a PSU incapable of handling this revised configuration, you would have to not only absorb the added cost of a PSU replacement, but also disassemble nearly your entire rig to reconnect all the replacement power cables to the components.

We are going to save our future selves a lot of unnecessary headaches and expenses and buy a PSU that will easily satisfy our equipment today while supporting a great deal of future hardware additions. I recommend going with the Corsair RM850 850-watt power supply.[2] The RM850 is 80 PLUS Gold

2.   http://www.corsair.com/us/power-supply-units/rm-series-power-supply-units/rm-series-rm850-80-plus-gold-certified-power-supply.html

Certified, meaning that it is highly energy efficient since the cooling fan spins only when there is a heavy load (when rendering high-end graphics, compressing data, and so on).

The RM850 is also fully modular, meaning that you only need to attach the power cables you need. Unlike cheaper PSUs that have a gangly wad of cables exploding out from the transformer box, the modular design of the RM850 will make cable management much easier. And when you do decide to install that beefy replacement graphics card in a few years, you won't need to find a Y-splitter to siphon power off of. Just plug another cable into the base of the RM850 like you would plug the cord of an electric appliance into a wall socket.

Besides being bundled with more than a dozen different cable types, another reason to go with the Corsair RM850 is because our PC case is from the same vendor. That gives us a high degree of confidence that our expensive PSU will fit snugly within the case and vent heat away without obstruction.

Installing the PSU

With our broad work area established, we're finally ready for the first step in building our PC! Unbox the PSU, account for all the parts, and lay it next to the case on the work surface.

Lay out the bags of cables and clips in an orderly fashion. Remember to discharge yourself from any static electrical buildup before mounting the PSU inside the case. And just as we did with the 500R PC case, we should verify that the RM850 box contains the advertised inventory, as Figure 3, *Make sure all parts are accounted for before installing the PSU*, on page 12 shows.

Remove both sides of the PC case using the top and bottom thumb screws on the rear of each panel. Slide the RM850 unit, with its fan facing down, into the lower-left corner of the case. The back of the RM850 should be facing the rear of the case. The PSU will sit on top of rubber spacers within the 500R case. These help correctly position the PSU as well as minimize noise from vibration. Check out Figure 4 on page 12, Figure 5 on page 13, and Figure 6 on page 13 to see how the RM850 PSU should be positioned and mounted inside the 500R PC case.

 If you opt to use a PC case other than the 500R, make sure there are venting holes on the bottom where the PSU is to be seated. Otherwise the PSU might overheat.

Figure 3—Make sure all parts are accounted for before installing the PSU.

Figure 4—The space inside the lower-left corner of the case, where the power supply will be mounted

Figure 5—The RM850 mounted inside the 500R PC case

Figure 6—The back of the mounted RM850

When you are satisfied with the orientation and position of the RM850 within the case, fasten the RM850 in place with the machine screws accompanying the power supply.

At this point, you may be tempted to plug in the PSU's power cable, flip the switch, and check if the PSU's bottom cooling fan turns on. If you tried, nothing would happen. That's because the PSU needs to be plugged into the motherboard first, which is what we will do in the next chapter.

Wrap-Up

Congratulations! You have just completed the first step of building your very own awesome PC! You also know what to look for when shopping for your own PC case and power supply. The importance of a clean, static-electricity-free work area also cannot be overstated. It will make your PC-building space much easier to move around, it'll be easier to organize your hardware, and it'll be less stressful.

In the next chapter we'll mount the CPU to the motherboard and the motherboard to the PC case. Then we will connect the case's front-panel wiring and the PSU's power cables to the motherboard. See you there!

CHAPTER 3

CPU and Motherboard

Now that we have a case to contain our PC parts and a power supply to electrify them, we're ready for the computer's heart and soul, the central processing unit (CPU) and motherboard (MOBO). These are the most important parts in a PC and they are also the most sensitive to damage. But as long as you take care in eliminating these variables from the equation, your CPU and MOBO installation and operation should proceed smoothly. As a reminder, you'll see the caution indicator next to the sections where you need to take extra care.

Speaking of steps, there are a lot to follow in this chapter. In addition to attaching the CPU to the MOBO, we will be mounting the MOBO inside the PC case. We'll also attach a cooling fan to keep the CPU from overheating. There are lots of wires to connect, so it's best to read through this chapter before tackling the assembly of your own PC. That way you will be better prepared to complete the challenging and delicate tasks discussed in this chapter. We will begin by choosing the CPU to use for our computer.

A CPU for Today and Tomorrow

For our PC build, I recommend basing the system on the Intel i7-4770K processor.[1] This very popular CPU represents the best price-for-performance value proposition. It runs at 3.5 GHz and can easily be overclocked (see *Overclocking*, on page 87, for more details) to run at speeds 3.9 GHz and faster. It has four cores, allowing today's multiprocessing applications such as high-end graphics programs, video editors, and complex games to run blazingly fast. In fact, most top game titles being released this year recommend using the i7-4770K CPU for ultra-level performance and compatibility.

---

1.   http://ark.intel.com/products/75123/Intel-Core-i7-4770K-Processor-8M-Cache-up-to-3_90-GHz

The i7-4770K also features integrated Intel HD graphics and supports hyperthreading. This allows the CPU to perform more than one task at a time. The CPU also supports efficient virtualization, which allows multiple operating systems to run simultaneously without conflicting with each other.

The 4770K chip is based on an LGA 1150 socket standard. This is important to know since you will need a motherboard that supports this socket size. Refer to the contents of the i7-4770K package in the next figure.

Figure 7—The Intel box contains the i7-4770K CPU, cooling fan, and instruction booklet.

We won't be using the CPU-cooling fan that comes with processor package. While the Intel fan is adequate for keeping the i7-4770K cool, it's loud and doesn't perform well should you decide to overclock the processor. In its place, we will use the Cooler Master Hyper N520 CPU cooler.[2] This dual-fan-based cooler features five copper heat pipes to rapidly dissipate the high temperatures generated by the i7-4770K.

Before we can mount the N520 CPU cooler, we have to install the CPU onto the motherboard. So let's take a look at what a motherboard does and which one we should use for our PC.

2.   http://www.coolermaster-usa.com/product.php?product_id=2879

A MOBO to House the CPU

A motherboard, MOBO for short, is the base where all power and components meet. The MOBO houses the CPU, RAM, GPU, and other peripheral cards. MOBOs have ports for data connections such as SATA, USB, and Ethernet. Sophisticated MOBOs also have onboard chips for audio, video, and wireless support. Good MOBOs are often more expensive than the CPUs they house, and the MOBO I recommend for our computer is no different.

When looking for the ideal motherboard, I knew from experience that I wanted excellent onboard audio and video, as well as Wi-Fi and Bluetooth so as not to be burdened with adding these essentials later. I also wanted a board capable of handling fast RAM, support for USB 3.0 and 6 GB/s SATA, and easy access to BIOS (Basic Input-Output System) settings and updates. And I wanted a MOBO that would be easy to convert to a water-cooled system should I decide to be more extreme with overclocking the CPU and GPU.

Based on these requirements, I recommend the ASUS Maximus VI Formula motherboard.[3] The Maximus VI Formula is an LGA 1150 socketed board designed to seat the i7-4770K CPU. It also houses an onboard Intel Z87 Express chipset to simultaneously handle up to six USB 3.0 and six SATA 6 GB/s ports. It can handle DDR3 RAM speeds up to 3,000 MHz, and it supports NVIDIA's SLI and AMD's three-way CFX video card linking technologies that potentially double the overall GPU performance.

ASUS also bundles software utilities that help with overclocking, controlling cooling fans with more granularity and helping optimize disk-drive performance.

Packed inside the Maximus VI Formula box are all the cables, fittings, and modules we will need to build out our PC, as Figure 8, *The contents of the Maximus VI Formula box*, on page 18 shows. No need to worry about not having enough SATA cables to connect our storage devices or the wrong type of fittings to attach hosing should we ever decide to water-cool the board (refer to *Water Cooling*, on page 90, for more details).

Remove all the items except for the motherboard from the box to easily verify that the full inventory of parts is included with the motherboard. With all parts accounted for, we are ready for our most serious step in the PC build process: fitting and clamping the CPU to the motherboard.

---

3.   http://www.asus.com/Motherboards/MAXIMUS_VI_FORMULA/

Figure 8—The contents of the Maximus VI Formula box

Installing the CPU

Like with all other steps involving electrical components, use caution when installing the CPU. You will be touching the brain and heart of the computer, and you can easily damage them if you're not careful. Some hardcore PC builders use antistatic shelves while standing on antistatic mats, wearing antistatic gloves when performing this step.

 If you can't guarantee a static-free environment, consider wearing an antistatic wrist strap to mitigate unexpected static-electricity discharges.

While those precautions might border on the extreme, the takeaway message is clear. Do not touch the CPU or motherboard until you are fully discharged (by touching metal such as the exposed unpainted interior of the 500R case, for example) and assembling while standing in a low-static environment, such as on a concrete or tiled floor. A healthy additional precaution is to wear an antistatic wrist strap if one is available, though it's not absolutely required.

 For this step, don't bother removing the motherboard from the box. Instead, just lift up the protective see-through packaging to expose the top of the motherboard. Locate the CPU socket on the motherboard. Look closely at the protective lid covering the LGA

1150 socket (as the next figure shows) and follow its instructions by not removing the lid. The lid will pop off by itself when you clamp the CPU into place.

Figure 9—The LGA 1150 CPU socket with protective plastic lid

Unhook the socket clamp and pull the arm back. This will lift the socket lid upward and expose the contact points where the socket pins on the MOBO will align and eventually touch the CPU contacts. Refer to Figure 10, *The LGA 1150 CPU socket exposed*, on page 20.

Remove the CPU chip from its plastic packing case and carefully place it into the newly exposed socket. Note that the CPU fits only one way into the socket (see Figure 11, *The i7-4770K CPU seated in the LGA 1150 socket*, on page 20). Two notches at the top of the CPUs circuit board will fit perfectly.

Ensure that the CPU is properly seated before clamping the lid shut. You can do this by gently sliding your finger up and down on the top of the CPU. If the CPU doesn't move around or slip, you're good to go.

Once the CPU is correctly positioned in the socket, press down on the arm to clamp the CPU to the MOBO and slide the notch of the socket clip under

Figure 10—The LGA 1150 CPU socket exposed

Figure 11—The i7-4770K CPU seated in the LGA 1150 socket.

the locking screw to keep the clamp in place. The protective plastic lid will pop off as you complete this step, as the next figure shows.

Figure 12—Clamping the CPU into place will pop off the CPU socket's protective plastic lid.

Check out your handiwork to see if it looks similar to the next figure. Congratulations—you have just completed one of the most important steps of a PC build!

Figure 13—The CPU securely seated and installed on the motherboard

Now that our CPU is firmly in place on the MOBO, we can install the motherboard into our PC case.

Seating the Motherboard

Remove both side panels of the 500R PC case such that the interior frame is completely exposed. Lay the PC case on its right side so it's easier to position the motherboard inside it (per the following figure).

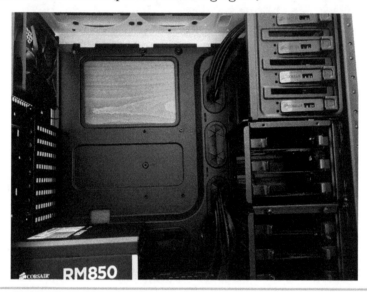

Figure 14—The exposed PC case is ready for MOBO mounting.

Before placing the motherboard inside the PC case, attach the plastic I/O port cover plate that accompanied the motherboard to the knocked-out I/O shield area in the upper-left side of the PC case, as Figure 15, *Snap the MOBO's I/O cover plate into this opening*, on page 23 shows.

Check the orientation of the plate within the rear cutout on the PC case so that the plate's openings line up with the MOBO I/O ports. Press the I/O cover against the PC case and the cover should click into place, per Figure 16, *Note the orientation and position of the mounted I/O cover*, on page 23.

 Ground yourself by touching a metal surface of the PSU before picking up the motherboard with clean hands. Pick up the motherboard along its sides and avoid touching the bottom of the MOBO. Gently position it over the nine mounting posts inside the PC case.

Figure 15—Snap the MOBO's I/O cover plate into this opening.

Figure 16—Note the orientation and position of the mounted I/O cover.

Check the alignment of the I/O ports to verify that they line up with the holes on the I/O plate we installed earlier. Once positioned, secure the MOBO to the mounting posts with the screws that accompanied the PC case, as shown in Figure 17, *The MOBO mounted in the PC case*, on page 24. Don't overtighten the screws. Doing so could snap off the screw heads as well as bend or crack the motherboard.

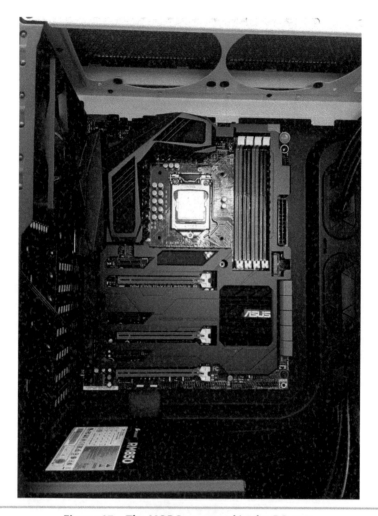

Figure 17—The MOBO mounted in the PC case

Complete the installation of the MOBO by attaching the mPCIe Combo II card between the motherboard and I/O shield, as Figure 18, *The mPCIe Combo II card*, on page 25 shows. This card is typically included in ASUS's high-end MOBOs, like its Maximus line. In addition to providing Bluetooth and Wi-Fi capabilities, the mPCIe card can house an M.2 (Next Generation Form Factor) solid-state drive (SSD) module for additional storage. Since we're going to use a more cost-effective 2.5" SSD, we will not be installing an M.2 SSD. This will leave the interior of the card vacant for now. You can purchase and install an M.2 SSD at a later time when you need additional solid-state storage in a small form factor.

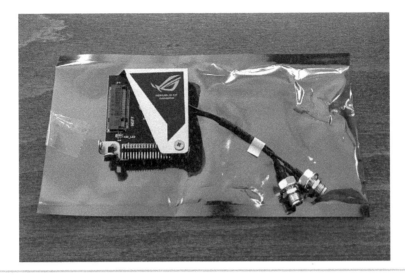

Figure 18—The mPCIe Combo II card

Remove the small screw on the module's bracket and align the mPCIe's connector with the corresponding port near the top left of the MOBO. Mount the card into the corresponding connector on the MOBO, as shown in the following figure.

Figure 19—The mPCIe Combo II card mounted on the MOBO

Secure the card in place by threading the mounting screw between the opening on the I/O plate we snapped into the case earlier and the mPCIe top screw hole on the card's bracket. Then thread the two Wi-Fi antenna connector wires into the matching port holes on the I/O cover. It doesn't matter which wire goes in which port hole. Tighten the bolt outside of the case by hand to secure both antenna connectors into position, as the next figure shows.

Figure 20—The I/O cover with all exposed ports aligned and secured

We're nearly finished with the hard stuff, but we still have one more jaw-clenching procedure to perform before we can hook up the power supply to the motherboard. We need to make sure that the powered CPU keeps its cool.

Installing the CPU-Cooling Unit

The heat generated by the i7-4770K (and most other modern-day PC CPUs) is intense. If you were to electrify your MOBO and touch the CPU while powering up, you would burn your finger within a few seconds of contact. In addition to damaging you, this heat will damage the CPU and MOBO. So it's critical that we install a component to safely dissipate that heat.

Rather than go with a more expensive and advanced water-cooling option, I decided to keep things simple with this PC build by taking a more traditional fan-based cooling approach. While the fans can generate more noise than a water-cooled approach, they are far cheaper and consistently proven to adequately cool the CPU. If you have no plans for trying to overclock the CPU, save yourself a few dollars and install the CPU fan bundled with the i7-4770K. It's adequate for the job and obviously engineered by Intel to cool its CPU. But it's designed for average operation in an average PC. We're building a high-end PC, so average just won't do. That's why I chose the Cooler Master Hyper N520 to perform the function of cooling down our hot CPU.

The Hyper N520 features five copper cooling pipes that connect to large aluminum plates attached to two fans to quickly dissipate the heat generated by the CPU (refer to the next figure). Its assembly is far larger than the stock CPU fan that Intel ships with the i7-4770K. Its larger size also makes attaching the fan to the motherboard slightly cumbersome. You need to be extra cautious and patient during the installation as a result.

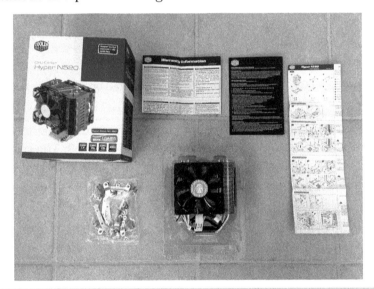

Figure 21—The contents of the Hyper N520 CPU fan package

The fan also comes with two types of bottom brackets that go on the back of the motherboard to anchor the fan firmly on top of the CPU. One bracket is for AMD CPUs while the one we're interested in is for Intel LGA 1150 CPU sockets. This socket size requires us to attach the two LGA 1150–sized side brackets to the base of the Hyper N520. Remove the protective plastic film from the copper base and align and mount the side brackets one at a time. Do so with the spring-loaded mounting screws facing down from the main body of the cooling fan, as shown in Figure 22, *LGA 1150-sized side brackets mounted on the Hyper N520*, on page 28.

Figure 22—LGA 1150-sized side brackets mounted on the Hyper N520

Note the four drill holes on the motherboard surrounding the CPU socket. This is where we will position the posts of the Hyper N520. The rear bracket sized for the LGA 1150–style socket will be on the back side of the mother-board, holding the mounted fan in place. But before we attach the Hyper N520 to the motherboard, we have to complete a very important step!

The square top of our CPU will be covered by the square bottom copper plate of the CPU fan. But while heat will transfer from a hot aluminum surface to a cooler cooper surface, the efficiency is reduced due to the gap between the two metals and the drop in conductivity due to the change in surface types. To greatly improve the effectiveness of heat transfer, we need to apply thermal paste to the top of the CPU before positioning the copper plate of the N520 over the CPU. This paste fills in any irregularities on the surface of the CPU cover and the cooling fan's contact plate, thereby ensuring the most efficient heat transfer between the two surfaces.

As you saw with the unboxing of the Hyper N520, the package included a tube of thermal paste. While this may be adequate for most, I found it to be a bit too fluid for my comfort. I have always had great success with Arctic Silver 5 high-density polysynthetic thermal paste.[4] Purchasing a tube adds

---

4.   http://www.arcticsilver.com/as5.htm

roughly $10 to the overall cost of the PC build, but that expense is worth the peace of mind of using a high-quality cooling compound.

True to its name, Arctic Silver contains silver, an excellent conductor of heat. It is also a highly sticky substance that you don't want to have land on anything but the top of the CPU cover.

Several schools of thought exist when applying thermal paste. Some prefer a drop the size of a pea while others prefer the size of a grain of rice. Some use a putty knife or the edge of a credit card to spread that amount evenly across the surface of the CPU top cover. Others let the CPU fan's connecting surface spread the paste when sandwiched between the CPU and the fan's connecting flat metal surfaces. I have used the latter approach for years without incident. I shy away from the spreading method so as not to accidentally sandwich any foreign materials in between the CPU and fan surfaces.

Before squeezing out a pea-sized dollop of Arctic Silver in the middle of the CPU cover, test squeezing out the measurement on a paper plate. This will give you a sense of how much pressure to apply to the syringe while voiding out any de-coagulated fluids that may have settled near the tip during shipment. When you're confident of your measurement and squeezing technique, place a small amount of Arctic Silver onto the CPU cover. Refer to the following figure for details.

Figure 23—A pea-sized drop of Arctic Silver on the CPU cover

Be careful not to overuse the thermal paste.

Carefully position the base of the Hyper N520 on top of the CPU (as you see in the next figure), allowing the weight of the copper base to evenly distribute the paste in between the two metal plates. Try not to pull apart the sandwich and change the orientation of the plates once each side has touched the thermal paste, as this could introduce unwanted pockets of air in between. Also be very careful not to allow the paste to ooze beyond the boundary of the two metal surfaces. If the conductive paste touches areas it's not supposed to be on, it could short out your CPU or motherboard. Should any excess paste bleed from the sides of the thermal sandwich, wipe it away using a cotton swab slightly dampened with rubbing alcohol.

Figure 24—Note the orientation of the Hyper N520 correctly mounted on the MOBO.

When you're satisfied with the position of the fan, thread the mounting screws into the LGA 1150 mounting plate placed on the back of the MOBO. The rear area of the PC case exposes the back portion of the MOBO explicitly so that the CPU-cooling fan's mounting plate can be installed. Position the rear mounting plate so that the four arms are flat against the back of the MOBO. You will see that the metal surfaces of the mounting plate are protected by insulating tape so that the mounting plate's metal does not touch the metal traces on the MOBO. Refer to the next figure for details.

Figure 25—The Hyper N520's mounting plate on the back of the motherboard

Reposition the mounting screws toward the middle of the mounting posts (they can slide into three different positions to accommodate different-sized sockets). Doing so will align the screws with the CPU-fan mounting holes on the MOBO. Tighten the nuts around each mounting screw, starting with the upper left and lower right, followed by the upper right and lower left. This will help maintain an evenly distributed amount of tension on the clamp and motherboard as you tighten the mounting screws. Be sure the fan is firmly in place and doesn't wiggle or slide once attached, but don't overtighten the mounting screws or you might bend and damage the motherboard.

The last item on the CPU-fan installation checklist is to plug the fan's wires into the CPU fan power plugs on the motherboard. The CPU fan power connectors are located to the upper right of the CPU socket on the MOBO. Cooler Master ships the N520 with both fan power wires attached to a Y-splitter. This allows both cooling fans to be powered by a single CPU fan connector on the motherboard. The drawback is both fans will always be on or off, running at the same speed. This limits the ability to control the speed of each fan independently. Fortunately, the Maximus VI Formula has two CPU-fan power connectors. So disconnect the longer of the two fan wires attached to the Y-splitter and plug each fan wire into the two available fan-connector slots.

With the mounting of the CPU fan onto the motherboard, you are nearly done with the most difficult, time-consuming portion of a PC build. All that is left to do with the motherboard is to connect the remaining case fans and power and data cables to it. Let's start with the fan and front-panel data cables.

Connecting the Cables

 Leave the power supply unplugged until your PC is ready to be powered on at the end of the build. We don't want any voltage going through the system unexpectedly during assembly.

Take a look at the front of PC case. See the openings for headphones, a microphone, USB, and even an old FireWire port? There's also an LED activity light for power state and hard drive activity as well as a few buttons to manage power state, as the next figure shows.

Figure 26—The front panel of the PC case

Now take a look in back of the panel and you will see a bundle of wires leading from those front-panel connectors. In order for the buttons and data connectors to do their job, we need to attach them to their appropriate connections on the motherboard. Normally this is done by reading the manual that accompanies a motherboard and determining which pins are associated with which wire. Fortunately, ASUS makes this easier by including a pin block (marketed as a Q-Connector) that aggregates the various front-panel power buttons and indicator-light wires into a single connector that plugs into the MOBO.

Take the end of the front-panel wires and plug the HDD LED, POWER SW, and RESET SW, along with the +P LED and -P LED wires, into the labeled pins on the Q-Connector. Check your pin configuration with the next two figures.

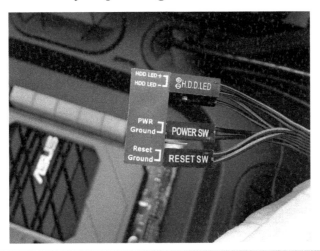

Figure 27—The front of the Q-Connector with HDD, POWER SW, and RESET SW wires connected

Figure 28—The back of the Q-Connector with -PLED and +PLED wires connected

Plug the Q-Connector into the associated pins on the motherboard. If you look closely at the bottom of the Q-Connector, you will see that most of the pins have corresponding holes but a few are covered. This is done to force you to correctly align the Q-Connector to the pins on the motherboard.

Next up are the wires for the front-panel audio jacks. This is a bit easier as these wires are already attached to a plug labeled HD AUDIO. Locate the corresponding plug on the motherboard (toward the bottom-left corner) and connect the HD AUDIO plug. Like the Q-Connector, the HD AUDIO plug connects only one way. Verify your plug orientation with the following figure.

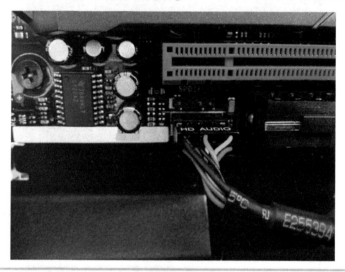

Figure 29—The PC case's HD audio cable plugged into the audio connector on the motherboard

Another important cable to plug into the motherboard from the PC case's front-panel ports is the USB 3.0 cable. Plug the end of this cable into the 20-pin USB 3.0 connector located toward the upper middle of the right side of the motherboard. Refer to Figure 30, *The 20-pin USB 3.0 connector on the MOBO*, on page 35.

Last, we need to connect the wires from the two fans on the front of the PC case to the motherboard. In addition to helping circulate air around the interior of the PC case, these fans have LEDs that can be lit strictly for presentation purposes. You can toggle these lights on and off via the lamp button on the PC case's front panel. You can also increase fan speed via a three-position slider switch to the right of the lamp button.

Figure 30—The 20-pin USB 3.0 connector on the MOBO

The fan wiring converges into a large four-pin plastic connector called a Molex connector. You've seen the male counterpart of this in one of the cable types that accompanied the RM850 PSU. In fact, the RM850 ships with duplicate sets of these cables, as the next figure shows.

Figure 31—Two sets of four-pin Molex connector power cables, one of which can be used to connect power to the side and front case fans

Plug the four-pin Molex male connector into the corresponding front-fan female adapter. Then plug the other end of the power cable into the RM850 base unit. As for the side fan, we could connect it now but the attached wire might get in the way of the rest of the build. Instead we will connect this freestanding four-pin plug when we're done with the build and ready to put the sides back onto the PC case.

We have one more built-in case fan to power, that being the fan in the back of the case near the motherboard's I/O shield. Just as we did for the CPU fan, locate the end of the wire coming from the rear case fan and note its three-pin connector. Attach this connector to the four-pin CHA FAN three-pins near the rear of the motherboard. Refer to the next two figures showing the before-and-after view of the attached wire.

Figure 32—Attach the rear case fan wire from to the CHA FAN three-pins on the motherboard.

Figure 33—The rear case fan wire is connected and ready for a spin.

Now that our front panel and case fans are connected to their respective locations, we're ready to attach the big power cables to our motherboard. They're big because they power not only the motherboard, but nearly everything else connected to the computer, including disk drives, keyboards, mice, and even headphones.

Powering the Motherboard

To deliver power from the PSU to the MOBO, we need to connect two main power cables in between. The first connector we will plug in is the largest. It's also the one with the most pins, the 24-pin ATX connector, as the next figure shows.

Figure 34—The ATX power plug is a primary power connection between the power supply and the motherboard. Note the USB 3.0 cable (from the USB ports on the front of the PC case) below the ATX connector that we attached earlier.

Use the 24-pin ATX cable from the Corsair RM850 package to insert into the ATX connector on the motherboard, as Figure 35, *The ATX power cable attached to the motherboard*, on page 38 shows. While you could just let the power cables freely lay on top of the MOBO, wire grommet openings have been punched in the case explicitly for cable management. Use these grommets to thread the power cables between the motherboard and the power supply.

Figure 35—The ATX power cable attached to the motherboard

Plug the other end of the power cable into the ATX 24-pin connector labeled on the power supply, per the two following figures.

Figure 36—The 24-pin ATX connector on the power supply

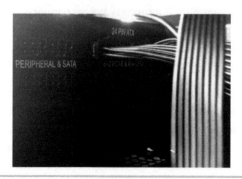

Figure 37—The ATX power cable attached to the power supply

Then connect the eight-pin eATX cable included in the RM850 PSU package from the eATX connector on the motherboard (located on the top left of the motherboard, near the mPCIe Combo II card that we installed previously) to the respective connector located on the PSU. Refer to Figure 38, Figure 39, and Figure 40 on page 40 for details. Remember to use the grommets punched in the case to thread the eATX cable behind the MOBO on the other side of the case. This way the power cable stays out of your way when attaching other components, such as RAM and graphics cards.

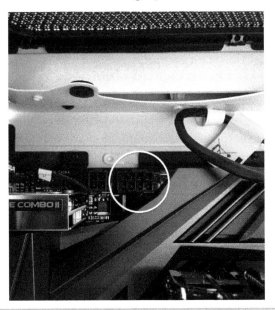

Figure 38—The eATX eight-pin connector on the motherboard

Figure 39—The eATX power cable attached to the motherboard

Figure 40—The eATX power cable attached to its respective port power supply

Phew! That was a lot of work, but fortunately the steps to finish the PC build are easier and come with less risk of damaging critical hardware during their installation.

You may have noticed that we have a few parts left over (refer to the following figure). That's typical given the modular approach to building your own PC. While they may look like junk, don't toss these spare parts out—they may come in handy one day.

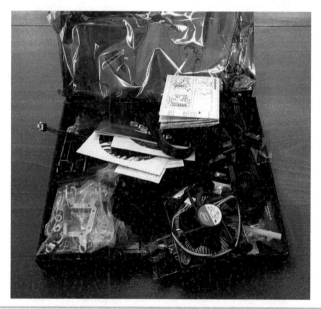

Figure 41—Hang on to leftover parts for expansion and remodeling purposes.

Wrap-Up

Nice job! You have just completed the most challenging aspect of building your own PC. You have connected the CPU to the MOBO and kept the CPU from overheating thanks to the CPU-cooling fan attachment. You have also connected the fans, front-panel controls, and power supply to the motherboard.

In the next chapter we will identify and attach our fast RAM and storage devices. The RAM will provide working memory space for PC applications to run, while our hard drives will give us long-term storage for our programs, media files, and other data.

CHAPTER 4

Memory and Storage

With the hardest part of building your PC completed, the remainder of the assembly is simply a matter of putting a few more parts together. But although doing this is easy, deciding which parts to use is where the challenge comes in. We are committed to building an awesome PC, so we need excellent components to complete our objective.

A key performance indicator in a computer, besides the speed of the CPU, is how quickly data can be fetched to move in and out of the CPU. The computer relies on storage to keep track of short- and long-term data. Short-term data is stored in random-access memory (RAM) while longer-term data (data that needs to survive after a system shuts down, for example) is stored on fixed media such as a solid-state drive (SSD) or hard-disk drive (HDD). Long-term data can also be stored on removable media such as DVD optical discs, though these devices are typically used for archival or physical-transport purposes. In this chapter we will be providing for all four storage types in our computer. We'll start with RAM.

RAM Speed and Performance

Just as there are different CPU sizes that fit into specific types of motherboard sockets, RAM modules are available in various configurations. The type of RAM that fits into our motherboard is known as *double data rate type three synchronous dynamic random-access memory*, or DDR3 SDRAM—DDR3 for short. The most prevalent data rate for DDR3 is 1,333 megatransfers per second (MT/s). That's a lot of data that can flow in a second, and while that's plenty fast for most PCs, we need something a bit peppier for ours.

Because our CPU and motherboard can handle the throughput thanks to the motherboard's support of Intel's Extreme Memory Profile (XMP), we are going for the gold by dialing our DDR3 RAM up to whopping 2,400 MT/s! Corsair will help us get there, with two sticks of Vengeance Pro 240-pin DDR3 2,400 MHz SDRAM,[1] giving us a total of 16 GB of SDRAM in our PC.

Like other DDR3 sticks, the Vengeance Pro has a notch offset from the center along the bottom connector pins. This notch aligns with a corresponding bump in the RAM slots on the motherboard, as the next figure shows.

Figure 42—The notch on the bottom of the SDRAM corresponds with the bump on the motherboard's SDRAM slot.

 Before installing the SDRAM, discharge yourself in the usual fashion before picking up the RAM with clean hands. Examine the RAM slots in the motherboard and make sure there is no dust or debris in the slots themselves.

Since we have only two RAM sticks to install for now, we'll insert the sticks into the red DDR3 (the first and third) slots on the motherboard. Why not use just any slot? Because we want the SDRAM to be paired in a dual-channel memory configuration.[2] This will allow us to read and write data on the SDRAM memory modules much faster.

Before insertion, unclip the white fasteners on the top of the slots. These clips, as shown in Figure 43, *Unfasten the white clips on the top of the SDRAM slots before installing the SDRAM sticks*, on page 45, will clamp onto the RAM and help lock it in place when the RAM sticks are properly inserted.

Align the notch on the bottom of the RAM stick with the bump in the RAM slot and push the RAM stick down evenly into the slot. It's a tight fit, so you

1. http://www.corsair.com/en-us/vengeance-pro-series-16gb-2-x-8gb-ddr3-dram-2400mhz-c10-memory-kit-cmy16gx3m2a2400c10r

2. http://en.wikipedia.org/wiki/Multi-channel_memory_architecture#Dual-channel_architecture

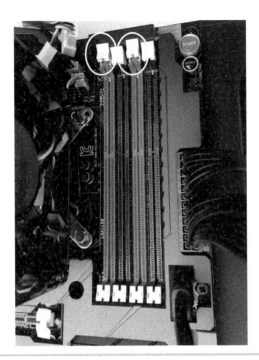

Figure 43—Unfasten the white clips on the top of the SDRAM slots before installing the SDRAM sticks.

may need to press firmly, but if you encounter a lot of resistance make sure you have correctly aligned the RAM. Pressing too hard could damage the RAM, the motherboard, or both.

As the RAM stick clicks into place, the white clip will clasp the notch on the side of the stick, locking it into place. Perform a final check to make sure all the contact pins along the bottom of the RAM stick are evenly aligned and seated into the RAM slot. When done, your seated SDRAM should look similar to Figure 44, *The SDRAM properly seated into the MOBO memory slots*, on page 46.

When you're ready to power on the computer and enter the Unified Extensible Firmware (UEFI) BIOS screen to configure your computer settings for the first time, you may be surprised to discover that the SDRAM speed is set to the default value of 1,333 MT/s. The system sets this initial value intentionally to ensure the widest range of compatibility with the different DDR3 RAM speeds and vendors. It's not until you set the XMP profile for the SDRAM in the BIOS configuration that you will be able to take advantage of the blazingly fast 2,400 MT/s speeds that the Vengeance Pro is capable of (we will touch

Figure 44—The SDRAM properly seated into the MOBO memory slots

on this further in *Overclocking*, on page 87). But we're not ready to turn the computer on just yet. We have to add long-term storage and a few other components first.

SSDs, HDDs, and DVDs

The two primary types of long-term storage today are solid-state drives and hard-disk drives. SSDs are superior to the older-technology HDDs because they have no moving parts and can read and write data much faster. However, SSDs are much more expensive than HDDs and do not yet hold the capacity that HDDs can. For this reason, we are going to combine the best of both technologies in our PC. We'll use an SSD to store our operating system and our most popular application files while we use an HDD to store our long-term large files such as games, videos, and other multimedia data.

Solid-State Drives

Like many of the hardware choices already made in this book, SSDs come in all different capacities and speeds. SSDs are also prone to failure if they are constantly writing data. Since we're going to use the drive primarily to install and run our operating-system files, I recommend spending the money for the

Samsung 250 GB 840 PRO Series SSD.[3] This is one of the most durable SSDs I've used and one of the fastest in its price class.

Installing the SSD requires four screws to mount the drive on one of the PC case's drive sleds. The screw holes are located on the bottom of the drive and need to be aligned with the holes on the bottom of the drive sled (as the next figure shows).

Figure 45—Use the four screw holes on the bottom of the drive to secure it to a drive sled.

You can choose any of the drive sleds seated in the drive bays to mount the SSD, but I chose the top drive bay as a visual indicator to remind me which drive is designated as the PC's primary boot drive. Remove the drive sled from the top drive bay by squeezing the drive sled's side tabs using your thumb and forefinger. The sled should unclip and slide right out, as shown in Figure 46, *Drive bays in the 500R PC case*, on page 48 and Figure 47, *Slide the drive sleds out to mount SSDs and HDDs onto them*, on page 48.

Using the four drive-bay screws that accompanied the 500R PC case, mount the SSD to the base of the drive sled, as shown in Figure 48, *The Samsung SSD mounted on the drive sled*, on page 49. The SATA data and power connectors should hang slightly past the edge of the sled. This will make it easier for us to plug the SATA and power cables into these connectors.

With the SSD securely mounted to the drive sled, slide the drive sled back into the drive bay until you hear and feel the sled clicking into place. All that's left for us to do with this drive is hook up the SATA and power cables. But before we do, let's mount our HDD and optical disc drives so we can plug them all in at the same time.

---

3. http://www.samsung.com/us/computer/solid-state-drives

Figure 46—Drive bays in the 500R PC case

Figure 47—Slide the drive sleds out to mount SSDs and HDDs onto them.

Figure 48—The Samsung SSD mounted on the drive sled

Hard-Disk Drives

My first hard-disk drive back in the 1980s was, at that time, a massive 20 MB and cost more than the combined components of the PC we're building! These days we can purchase 4 TB drives for well under $200. That's the size I recommend going with for our HDD, and I've been relatively satisfied with the reliability of Seagate hard drives.[4]

Mounting the 4 TB Seagate drive is far simpler than measuring the SSD because the PC case's drive bays are built for their 3.5" drive size. And just as before with the choice of drive bay for the SSD, you can choose any bay you like. I chose the bottom bay to visually distance what will be our secondary drive from our SSD primary drive.

Slide out the bottom drive-bay sled using the same thumb-and-forefinger-pinch technique. Then flex the sides of the sled far enough to clip the HDD into place—no screws required! Just like the SSD, the HDD SATA and power ports should hang slightly beyond the edge of the drive sled for easy access, as shown in Figure 49, *The 3.5" 4 TB hard drive mounted on the drive sled*, on page 50.

With the HDD securely clipped into the drive sled, slide the sled back into the drive bay. The last drive to mount into our PC is an optical disc drive.

Optical Disc Drives

This was a peripheral I struggled to include. Physical portable media like CD-ROMs, DVDs, and Blu-ray discs are vestiges from a time when the Internet

---

4. http://www.seagate.com/internal-hard-drives/desktop-hard-drives/desktop-hdd/

Figure 49—The 3.5" 4 TB hard drive mounted on the drive sled

was not as reliable or depended upon as it is today. But this physical optical-media legacy will continue for at least another 10 years, and some media (like high-resolution 3D movies) still almost exclusively ships on these discs.

Depending on what you plan on using your computer for, you can opt for something as basic as a read-writeable DVD drive or spend $40 more for a Blu-ray drive capable of playing Blu-ray movies. For the basic build, I chose an inexpensive ASUS DVD-ROM drive.[5]

Install the optical drive in any of the PC case's top drive bays. Be sure to clear the area of any stray wiring so it doesn't get pinched when inserting the optical drive into the bay; see Figure 50 on page 51.

I chose the top slot so that it's close to the case's front button panel and it looks nicer and more contiguous as a result. Installing an optical drive is slightly different from installing an HDD or SSD because the drive tray has to eject outward. So instead of installing the drive from the inside, we need to pop off the drive bay's cover by squeezing the plastic clips to release it (as shown in Figure 51 on page 51).

Slide the optical drive into the drive bay with the disc tray facing outward. Slide the drive in slowly and continue to push it into the bay until you feel and hear a click. The plastic clips on the side of the drive bay will lock and

---

Figure 50—The 500R case provides four front-facing drive bays.

Figure 51—Remove the top drive bay's cover from the inside by squeezing the side clips and pushing the cover out away from the case.

hold the drive in place. The front of the optical drive should be flush with the front of the PC case, as the next figure shows.

Figure 52—The DVD-ROM drive is correctly installed.

Now that our SSD, HDD, and optical drives are mounted, we need to connect the SATA data cables and power cables to each drive. Use the SATA cables that accompanied the Maximus VI motherboard, preferably the ones with the right-angle SATA connector. This type of cable will not stick out as much from the back of drive. Therefore, it will stay out of the way of other internal components and the side cover of our PC case. Insert the five-pin power connector that came with the RM850 power supply into the power port of each drive, as the next figure shows.

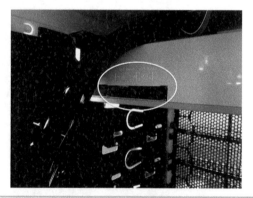

Figure 53—Insert a SATA and power cable into each installed drive.

Note that the five-pin power connector has several power plugs that you can use in a daisy chain to power multiple drives from a single wire (such as the SSD and HDD); see the next figure.

Figure 54—The SSD and HDD can be powered by a single power cable.

Plug the other end of the two power-cable connectors (one for the optical drive and the other for the daisy-chained SSD and HDD) into any of the peripheral ports in the RM850 PSU, as shown in the the following figure and in Figure 56, *The six-pin SATA power cables plugged into the RM850 PSU*, on page 54.

Figure 55—Connect the drive power cables into any available peripheral and SATA power ports on the PSU.

Figure 56—The six-pin SATA power cables plugged into the RM850 PSU

Last, we need to connect the SATA cables attached to the drives into the SATA ports on the motherboard. These are easy to identify on the MOBO, as they are bright red and in a bank of six ports on the right side of the motherboard, as seen in the following figure.

Figure 57—The Maximus VI Formula has 10 SATA 6 GB/s data connectors on the motherboard.

You can plug the SATA cables into any of these ports for the drives to work. In case you want to use a more advanced drive setup such as a RAID configuration, we will cover RAID in *RAID*, on page 88. For now, plug the SATA cables into the first three SATA connectors on the motherboard.

Make sure the SATA cable and power connections are well seated and pushed in all the way. Loose cable connections will bring instability, system glitches, and other weird problems. After you've checked all the cables for solid connectivity, your short- and long-term storage hookups are ready for use. Congratulations!

Wrap-Up

We have given our awesome PC's brain both short-term and long-term memory, and we're so close to flipping the power switch to bring our creation to life. If you're impatient, you could do that now if you have an HDMI-compliant display (any modern flat-panel television will do) via an HDMI cable connected from the display to the rear I/O HDMI port on the graphics card. But I prefer to have all the parts installed before experiencing the thrill of victory or the agony of defeat. So if you can, hold off plugging in the computer for just a little while longer.

In the next chapter we will install a high-end graphics card that pushes real-time image processing to the limit. We'll also take audio reproduction into consideration. Only a few more parts to install, and we'll be able to finally enjoy the fruits of our investment and hands-on labor.

CHAPTER 5

Sound and Video

When I built my first PC more than 25 years ago, the graphics were capable of displaying 16 colors onscreen. A few years later dedicated sound cards would allow the generation of sound beyond chiptune-style manipulation of the internal speaker. We have come a long way in a quarter of a century.

Today's PC audiovisual components are capable of rendering in milliseconds computer animation that took a room-sized computer weeks or more to calculate 40 years ago. Audio fidelity can now replicate high-end concert and moviegoing experiences. We are going to imbue our PC with both of these capabilities. Let's begin with audio.

Awesome Audio

PC audio has come a long way since the days of the first PCs, when hearing the bleeps and buzzes of an internal speaker was exciting. Today's PC audio can supply a theater quality–capable discrete surround-sound experience in clean digital audio fidelity. Let's consider some audio options.

Is a Sound Card Necessary?

Before high-quality audio was expected to be a standard feature on a personal computer, the only way you could reproduce high-quality digitized audio was via a sound card. However, as motherboard manufacturers like ASUS began to incorporate more features that were once separate add-ons, the need for a dedicated sound card greatly diminished. The motherboard we used to build our computer has exceptional audio that negates any reason to add a dedicated sound card.

The only reason worth considering a dedicated sound card today would be if you are an audio engineer who uses a PC to process professional-level sound for game or film production. But for our immediate needs of rendering home

cinema or distinct-audio-channel game-playing experiences, the audio technology onboard the Maximus VI motherboard delivers the goods. However,
we still need to send that audio to an end device that can render the sound
data with perfection.

Speakers and Headsets

The I/O ports provided by our motherboard can deliver to both analog and
digital speakers and headsets. While you certainly could use a cheap pair of
stereo speakers or a set of low-cost earbuds, it would be a waste of the
motherboard's audio-fidelity capabilities. To get the most out of the sound
data being emitted, use quality equipment that can handle it.

In the case of speakers, take advantage of the optical digital-audio output
capability that the Maximus VI provides. High-quality home theater and PC
speakers can plug directly into the Toshiba TOSLINK fiber-optic port located
on the motherboard's rear I/O panel. Doing so delivers crystal-clear digital
sound directly to the external amplifier to decode and send the output to the
speakers. The Logitech Speaker System Z906 is the best dedicated PC
speaker system I have heard that takes advantage of this configuration (check
it out in the next figure).[1] This Dolby 5.1 five-speaker system is THX certified,
meaning that the speakers can replicate the high-end movie-theater experience
in the home. The Z906 also provides multiple audio-input plugs to service
more than just the PC. Once you have heard the amazing clarity and channel
separation of these speakers even at high volume, you will never be able to
go back to using cheap stereo PC speakers again.

Figure 58—The THX-certified Logitech Speaker System Z906

1.   http://www.logitech.com/en-us/product/speaker-system-z906

However, there may be situations when you can't rattle the rafters. Whether it's out of consideration for family members, roommates, or neighbors complaining of the volume level, or your desire to combine headphones with a microphone for multiplayer gaming, a good set of headphones should also be on your shopping list. If you don't intend to use your PC for Internet voice calling, there are a number of excellent high-end stereo headphones available. But if you're like me and need to occasionally wear a headset for Skype or Google Hangout calls, consider Corsair's Vengeance 1500 Dolby 7.1 USB gaming headset (see the next figure). I find them to be high quality and comfortable; they fit my head well and don't cook my ears even during long calls.[2]

Figure 59—The Corsair Vengeance 1500 USB headset

While the motherboard's onboard audio will serve our needs nicely, the same can't be said of the onboard video. It's functional enough for basic use and troubleshooting, but for our PC to be truly awesome, we need a powerhouse video card to keep up with the computationally intensive demands of rendering modern entertainment in real time.

Pushing Pixels

Today's high-end graphics cards are often more powerful than the computers they are installed in. That's because they are performing a massive amount of real-time computation to render photorealistic images and animations

---

2.   http://www.corsair.com/en-us/vengeance-1500-dolby-7-1-usb-gaming-headset-v2

onscreen. The graphics processing unit (GPU) is a purpose-designed chipset that pipelines graphics data to make it seamlessly render display data.

Just like the CPU we installed earlier, high-end GPUs generate a lot of heat —so much that they require larger fans and thermal conductive metal surfaces to cool them down. And just like CPUs, high-end GPUs can be overclocked to push their rendering speeds. The faster they perform, the hotter they operate. When air cooling fails to adequately keep GPU operating temperatures at bay, most high-end cards accept water-cooled attachments to prevent overheating.

Two leading companies currently compete in the high-end consumer graphics-card market. AMD makes the Radeon series, and NVIDIA has its GeForce line of cards. Both companies have designed hardware that is quite capable of rendering today's most graphically intense games, support dual- and even triple-monitor setups, and can be chained together with identical cards to further boost graphic output. Choosing one or the other is strictly a personal preference, and I prefer the NVIDIA brand. I recommend the NVIDIA-powered ASUS GeForce GTX 780 Ti graphics card (which the next figure shows).[3] Several manufacturers make this card based on NVIDIA's reference implementation. Since we have an ASUS motherboard, it makes sense to go with an ASUS graphics card to ensure 100 percent hardware compatibility.

Figure 60—The ASUS GeForce GTX 780 Ti graphics card is a beautiful, beastly GPU!

---

3.   http://www.asus.com/Graphics_Cards/GTX780TI3GD5/

This is not NVIDIA's top-of-the-line card, but its GPU can be easily overclocked to match the speed of the company's best-in-class card, for several hundred dollars less.

Installing the Graphics Card

The GTX 780 Ti is a big card, taking up two expansion-card bays on the motherboard. It also plugs into the long PCIe slot, of which there are three on the Maximus VI. The two PCIe slots closest to the CPU communicate with the card at the fastest speeds possible, while the PCIe slot farthest from the CPU runs at half the speed of the other two long PCIe slots. Keep this in mind if you ever want to buy a second GTX 780 Ti and want to daisy-chain them together to make what NVIDIA calls a Scalable Link Interface (SLI) connection.

Since we're going to start with a single graphics card, we will install it in the PCIe slot closest to the CPU on the motherboard. This not only makes it easier for us to install a second GTX 780 Ti later on, but it also keeps the cooling fan on the side of the card unobstructed.

Before inserting the card into the long PCIe slot, remove the two expansion-slot covers on the PC case that match where the graphics card will be mounted. This should be the second and third slot covers, as shown in the following figure and in Figure 62, *Remove the second and third slot covers to accommodate the graphics card*, on page 62.

Figure 61—These are the PC-case slot covers.

Figure 62—Remove the second and third slot covers to accommodate the graphics card.

With the card-slot covers removed, prepare the PCIe slot for insertion by making sure the expansion slot's white locking tab is slid back to accommodate the three-sectioned connector on the bottom of the graphics card.

 Position the video ports on the front of the card so they are accessible through the two slots we removed the covers from. Align the connector on the bottom of the card with the PCIe slot. Then slowly yet firmly seat the card into the slot.

You should feel and hear the slot's plastic locking tab click into place, securing the card to the expansion slot. Refer to Figure 63, *The GTX 780 Ti card mounted in the PCIe expansion slot on the motherboard*, on page 63 for how the card should look once properly mounted in the expansion slot.

Powering the Graphics Card

As mentioned earlier, the GTX 780 Ti is power-hungry. It has to be in order to deliver the high frame rates and real-time rendering pipelines it can achieve. It also has a large cooling fan to keep the GPU's temperature in check. Therefore, in addition to the power it receives via its PCIe connection to the motherboard, the GTX 780 Ti has two additional power connectors (an eight-pin and a six-pin) on the top back of the card, as shown in Figure 64, *The GeForce GTX 780 Ti requires a lot of electricity to power it*, on page 63.

Grab the two appropriate six- and eight-pin cable types from the bundle included with the RM850. Plug them into the case and then into the PSU, as shown in Figure 65, *The GeForce GTX is plugged in, powered, and ready to run*, on page 63.

Figure 63—The GTX 780 Ti card mounted in the PCIe expansion slot on the motherboard

Figure 64—The GeForce GTX 780 Ti requires a lot of electricity to power it.

Figure 65—The GeForce GTX is plugged in, powered, and ready to run.

Now that the graphics card's data and power connections are hooked up, we can close the PC case by putting the two sides back on. Recall that we have to plug the side fan into the available four-pin power adapter mentioned toward the conclusion of the section *Installing the CPU-Cooling Unit*, on page 26. With the side fan powered and the PC case closed up, we can connect a display to the graphics card to see the beautiful imagery that the GTX 780 Ti generates.

Displaying the Graphics

The GTX 780 Ti has four graphics output ports: two DVI ports, an HDMI port, and a DisplayPort. This technically allows the card to simultaneously output graphics to four separate displays. Doing so can make for some very interesting monitor configurations. For example, you could connect a desktop monitor to a DVI port for computing by day and a flat-panel TV to the HDMI port for evening entertainment. Some people have even connected three monitors of the same size and resolution on their desk while mounting a flat-panel TV on a wall just above the three monitors.

I have tried a number of monitor variations, often settling on two for my software-development purposes (one to display my code and the other to show my running application). But for gaming and watching movies, I find the side-by-side bezels of a multimonitor setup incredibly annoying. Given the falling prices of high-resolution flat-panel computer monitors, you can buy a 29" display for much less than the cost of two 19" displays.

Two popular types of flat-panel monitors on the market today are LED and IPS. LED is more prevalent and less expensive, but can't match the viewing angles or dynamic contrast of IPS. But if you're a gamer, IPS may not be ideal since its lower refresh rates can cause ghosting or smearing of high-speed action onscreen. IPS is ideal for computer-aided design (CAD) and graphic-design work.

Being more a gamer than a graphic designer, I chose the 27" BenQ XL2720T model for my monitor of choice (see Figure 66, *The BenQ XL2720T 27" display*, on page 65).[4] In addition to its sleek look and small-footprint stand, the XL2720T features customizable viewing preferences and aspect ratios in multiple resolutions, up to 1920×1080. Its high 120Hz refresh rate has lightning-fast 1 millisecond pixel-display response times and also supports NVIDIA's 3D Vision 2 for 3D viewing entertainment.

---

4.   http://gaming.benq.com/gaming-monitor/xl2720t

Figure 66—The BenQ XL2720T 27" display

One often-overlooked but very important feature that the XL2720T has is a pivoting height-adjustable and tiltable arm—no more stacks of books required under the base of a monitor to elevate the screen to an ergonomically healthy level. Oh, and there's a hook on the back of the monitor to hang your headset and keep it from tangling on your desk.

Connecting the monitor to the computer is as simple as plugging the supplied DVI cable into either one of the available DVI ports on the GTX 780 Ti. The monitor also supports HDMI and DisplayPort inputs, but using those requires the purchase of a separate cable.

Wrap-Up

Installing a graphics card and connecting it to a monitor was pretty easy. Connecting speakers to our motherboard's audio I/O ports was even easier. In the next chapter we'll attach the easiest yet most important devices in a modern computer. Without a mouse and keyboard, we won't get very far on the BIOS configuration screen that we see when we turn on the computer for the first time.

In addition to considering which mouse and keyboard to use with our PC, we'll take a brief look at some additional peripherals in the next chapter. These enhancements may not be essential to operating our PC, but they sure will make using the PC an even more awesome experience!

CHAPTER 6

Keyboard, Mouse, and Other Peripherals

Our awesome PC is built. We attached the side panels, connected our speakers and display, and plugged in the power cable, and we're ready to flip the switch. While we certainly could do that, we wouldn't get very far. That's because when we turn on the computer for the very first time, the UEFI BIOS that bootstraps the entire computer would ask us to press any key to continue. In order to do that, we need a keyboard connected. And since the Maximus VI Formula motherboard has a graphical user interface, a mouse should also be connected to effortlessly navigate around the UEFI BIOS settings.

In addition to a keyboard and mouse, we will consider a few entertainment-related peripherals. These include 3D hardware to take advantage of the BenQ NVIDIA 3D Vision 2 compatibility, a racing rig for driving simulations, and a peek into world of virtual reality with the help of the Oculus Rift virtual-reality headset.

Keyboard

Computer keyboards (and mice, for that matter) are extremely subjective and very personal devices. It is with this collection of plastic and metal that we users connect with our PCs. A keyboard is the original computer touch interface and, quite frankly, not much has changed with its design since its inception.

Historically descended from the QWERTY typewriter, the original keyboard that shipped with the famed IBM PC from the 1980s was a solid and well-built peripheral. For those old enough to recall using one, the distinctive aspect of the keyboard was its finely tuned click-clack response of pressing the keys. As the PC became more commoditized, the materials used to construct the keyboard became cheaper. Cost often overrode quality and plenty of junky keyboards were manufactured and sold as a result.

Fortunately, a market for quality keyboards still exists. While most of these companies cater to hard-core PC gamers, any PC user can benefit from these precision-honed keyboard offerings. For our PC, I recommend using Corsair's Vengeance K95 keyboard.[1] While its high price may make some consider alternatives, I have yet to use a PC keyboard that matches the build quality and feature set that the K95 delivers. Click-clack is back, with more sensitivity and less noise courtesy of the K95's use of Cherry MX Red switches on every key. The keyboard has individual LEDs to light up every key on the keyboard, and these LEDs can be programmed to turn on and off and saved as a preset. This feature has helped me not only with games, but also when learning a new text editor or application with keyboard shortcuts. The same goes for the 18 macro keys on the left side of the keyboard. You can assign a string of keypresses to a single macro key, further reducing the number of keypresses to achieve your typing objectives.

Colorful Keyboard Switches

Besides Cherry MX Red keyboard switches, there are also Blue, Green, Brown, Black, Clear, and ALPS designations. Blue, Brown, Black, and Red are among the most popular.

Red has the softest downstroke and isn't tactile, meaning that you won't feel a noticeable click during the downstroke of a keypress. Black is similar to Red except that the keys are slightly harder to press down. Blue is also popular since it is a tactile switch type. Brown is almost identical to Blue, but the click occurs sooner on the downstroke, giving you further tactile notice ahead of committing to a full keypress.

Installing the keyboard is simple. Plug the two keyboard USB cables into an available USB port on the rear I/O panel. I suggest using the standard USB 2.0 ports (the ones without the blue plastic tab inside the port) since the K95 and nearly all other PC keyboards on the market do not need the throughput speeds of USB 3.0 to operate. And yes, I did say plug the two keyboard USB cables into the rear I/O panel. One handles the keypress data and the other powers the keyboard LEDs.

You won't be able to take advantage of the K95's programmable features until you install the Microsoft Windows operating system. Corsair provides keyboard drivers only for Windows, so if you plan on installing a different OS on your computer, you may want to consider using a model other than the K95.

---

1.   http://www.corsair.com/en-us/vengeance-k95-fully-mechanical-gaming-keyboard

Mouse

Just like the computer keyboard, choosing the right PC mouse is a subjective decision. Many factors need to be considered, such as the size of your hands, the type of surface you plan on using the mouse on, the number of mouse buttons, color, tracking resolution, and so on.

Partly due to a desire to stay within the same product family and color, and partly because I really like the comprehensive number of programmable features, I chose the Corsair Vengeance M95 mouse for our PC.[2] This mouse is not for those who like simple, smooth two-button mouse operation. The M95, like its K95 counterpart, is decked out with buttons that can be pressed to string together multiple commands. And like the K95, these mouse-button macros can be stored onboard or saved to a file for different user-scenario configurations.

For example, I created a mouse profile for programming that allows me to launch global finds and code bookmark searches with a single click of one of the M95's side buttons. Likewise, I reconfigured the mouse for quickly accessing the various stances an onscreen character can take in games like Arma III or Dayz.[3,4]

You can plug the M95 into an available USB port on your PC, but I suggest taking advantage of the available USB port on the back of the K95, which was designed for this purpose (as demonstrated in Figure 67, *Plug the M95 into the USB port on the back of the K95*, on page 70). This helps make up for the fact that the keyboard is using two USB ports. And as is the case with the K95, the M95 software that drives the mouse is designed exclusively for use with Microsoft Windows. Both the K95 and the M95 will operate as expected on non-Windows platforms, but you won't be able to create and store macros, programmatically control the LEDs, or upgrade the firmware in these peripherals without their accompanying Windows drivers.

The last accessory to add to the Corsair-centric keyboard-and-mouse combination is the Vengeance MM200 Gaming Mouse Mat – Extended Edition.[5] This is more than just a generic mouse mat. The MM200 spans the full width of the keyboard and mouse working area. I find it a vastly better setup than using a standalone mouse pad that tends to get pushed out of place with

---

2. http://www.corsair.com/en-us/vengeance-m95-performance-mmo-and-rts-laser-gaming-mouse-gunmetal-black

3. http://www.arma3.com

4. http://dayzgame.com

5. http://www.corsair.com/en-us/corsair-mm200-gaming-mouse-mat-extended-edition

Figure 67—Plug the M95 into the USB port on the back of the K95.

heavy mouse use. Some mouse mats use thick rubber padding that elevates the mouse higher than the keyboard, making long-term mouse use uncomfortable. By using a continuous mat underneath the keyboard and mouse, both peripherals remain in place at the same elevation. Plus, as you can see in the next figure, the Corsair K95/M95/MM200 combination just looks cool.

Figure 68—The K95 keyboard and M95 mouse resting on the MM200 mouse mat

We now have everything we need attached to our PC to turn it on. So before we continue looking at peripherals, let's do just that.

The Moment of Truth

The time has come to see if what we built is truly as awesome as we want it to be. Make sure your monitor's power cable is plugged in and press the touch-sensitive power button on the front lower-right corner to turn on the monitor. Plug the power cable into the PC's power supply, turn the power-supply switch on, and press the power button on the front panel of the PC case. If everything was assembled and connected correctly, you should hear the internal fans whir and see your monitor flicker to life in a few seconds. On the initial boot screen, you should see the message "New CPU installed! Press enter Setup to configure your system. Press F1 to Run SETUP." Pressing the F1 key will bring you to the UEFI BIOS settings screen shown in the figure. Choose to view the EZ Mode to see a snapshot of your hardware, similar to the example in the figure.

Figure 69—The UEFI BIOS Utility EZ Mode screen

For now, accept the default values by pressing the Esc key on the keyboard, then scroll to select the Save and Exit option. This will save the default hardware-configuration settings and apply those settings each time the computer boots up. We will change these settings later on, but for now the defaults will get us far enough along to install an operating system. We will do that in the next chapter.

Before we install an operating system, let's take a brief look at some of the most exciting PC peripherals available today.

The Fun Stuff

Now that you have working PC hardware, you can reward yourself with some accessories that will provide a bit of virtual rest and relaxation. None of the peripherals discussed in this section are vital to your enjoyment of your new

> ### Joe asks:
> ## What If the PC Doesn't Work?
>
> The most common explanation for a newly built computer not powering up is a simple lack of power. If you see no indication of power whatsoever (no indicator lights glowing on the motherboard, cooling fans not spinning, and so on), first check to make sure you correctly plugged the power cable from the power supply into a working electric wall socket. If that checks out, make sure the switch on the back of the power supply is flipped to the on position and try pressing the front panel's power button again. These verification checks resolve the power problem most of the time.
>
> If you still don't see any indication of the PC receiving power, remove the side panels and trace the front-panel wiring to make sure everything connects in the right place. Sometimes a wire can get knocked loose while shuffling cables and drives. Also verify that the graphics card and SDRAM are properly seated. If everything appears to be correctly hooked up, there is the very small possibility that you have a defective power supply. If you suspect this to be the case, contact the manufacturer (in our case, Corsair) for help troubleshooting the power supply and determining if it needs to be replaced.

PC. However, they do elevate the enthusiasm factor and prove to be good showcases for demonstrating your new computer's power.

3D Glasses

Because you installed a high-end graphics card driven by NVIDIA technology and a 3D-compatible monitor, you can add an accessory that will turn your 2D-screen viewing experience into a 3D wonder. The NVIDIA 3D Vision 2 Wireless Glasses Kit includes a wireless infrared transmitter, a few connection cables, and one pair of active LCD stereoscopic glasses, as shown in Figure 70, *NVIDIA's 3D Vision 2 kit*, on page 73.[6]

Configuring the kit is as simple as downloading and installing the latest 3D Vision 2 drivers from NVIDIA's website, plugging in the USB cable connecting the computer to the 3D Vision 2 infrared emitter, and pressing the power button on the left side of the 3D Vision 2 glasses. You're ready to play 3D content on your computer.

Even though the hype train for 3D games and movies left the station years ago, the technology is still rather impressive for those immune to the side-effects that the glasses can have on some people. I have no problems wearing

---

6. http://www.nvidia.com/object/product-geforce-3d-vision2-wireless-glasses-kit-us.html

Figure 70—NVIDIA's 3D Vision 2 kit

them for a long time, while my best friend can stomach them for only a few minutes before the effect induces an acute headache.

If you're the only person who will use the glasses to watch movies or play games, this kit has everything you need. But if you want to watch the 3D content together with a friend or family member, you will have to buy a second pair of NVIDIA's 3D glasses, which is nearly two-thirds the cost of the full 3D Vision 2 kit.

The final consideration on whether to pay for the privilege of 3D viewing on your PC is the fact that 3D is no longer enthusiastically supported in the marketplace. Only a trickle of 3D blockbuster movies are released in Blu-ray 3D format and almost no new games in development are being designed to specifically take advantage of NVIDIA's 3D kit. Even so, there are more than 600 existing titles that range from meager to excellent 3D-supported reproduction. And there is also video-playback software (which I'll mention in the next section) that can do a surprisingly decent job of converting 2D video into 3D imagery. Watching old family home videos in this way brings an exhilarating feeling of traveling back in time to be an immersed historical spectator.

Blu-ray Drive

The other part of the equation for taking full advantage of 3D glasses is the ability to play back 3D movies. Since 3D movies are really two movies playing back at the same time (one movie for each eye), Blu-ray optical discs are the go-to playback media since they have the capacity (and digital copy protection) to make physical distribution of this content possible.

Not all Blu-ray players built for use in PCs will play Blu-ray 3D discs. Some of the less expensive models are not even intended for media playback, but just for disc burning. For this reason, I recommend the LG WH14NS40 Blu-ray drive (as seen in the next figure).[7] It might not be the fastest disc-burning drive on the market, but it supports all the major Blu-ray media formats, including 3D.

Figure 71—LG's WH14NS40 Blu-ray drive

Installing the Blu-ray drive is identical to the steps we followed for the DVD-ROM drive installation. Swapping out an existing DVD-ROM with a Blu-ray drive takes only a minute since you already have all the cables in place. You don't even have to unscrew anything, since we used the side clamps built into the PC case's drive bay to secure the DVD-ROM drive earlier. Unhook the cables and squeeze the clamps to release the old DVD-ROM drive. Then slide the old drive out from the front of the PC case, and slide the new Blu-ray drive in until you feel the click of the side clamps holding the drive in place. Connect the SATA and power cables to the back of the Blu-ray drive, and you're ready to go.

Operating systems like Linux or Microsoft Windows 8.1 do not include built-in support for Blu-ray movie playback, so you need a Blu-ray-playback application to watch Blu-ray movies on your PC. I recommend PowerDVD Ultra since it can be used to play back both Blu-ray and Blu-ray 3D discs.[8] The program also supports the new Ultra HD 4K video format for when you're ready to make the leap to a display capable of showing resolutions of 3,840

7.   http://www.lg.com/us/data-storage/lg-WH14NS40

8.   http://www.cyberlink.com/products/powerdvd-ultra

pixels by 2,160 lines (and as high as 7,680 pixels by 4,320 lines for Ultra HD quality). It will be a few more years before Ultra HD video content becomes the norm, so your current 1080p monitor will be quite adequate for some time.

Racing Wheel

A racing-wheel peripheral is a true luxury for auto-racing-simulation enthusiasts. The Logitech G27 Racing Wheel is the best I've used in its price range.[9] The force feedback brings an elevated feeling of immersion and the leather steering wheel and gearshift hood ooze quality. Of course, if you're not a fan of racing games, acquiring this expensive peripheral is hard to justify. But if you love driving and tinkering with cars as much as you love building and tinkering with PCs, the G27 (shown in the following figure) makes driving games a blast to play.

Figure 72—Logitech's G27 Racing Wheel

Game Controllers

For the gaming generalist looking to emulate a gaming-console experience on the PC, a number of gamepads exist. These controllers range from cheap plastic to solid gold in terms of quality, but the game controller I consistently reach for when playing platform-style games is Microsoft's Xbox 360 Controller

---

9. http://gaming.logitech.com/en-us/product/g27-racing-wheel

for Windows.[10] As the product name implies, it's an Xbox 360 controller designed to work with Microsoft Windows games. The controller is available in both a wired and, for about $20 more, a wireless version. I use the wired version since I don't play a lot of platform titles that require the use of a game controller. The wired version (which the next figure shows) has enough length in the cable to reach around most desktop PC setups.

Figure 73—The Xbox 360 wired controller for Windows

For flight-simulation enthusiasts, a well-constructed joystick with a heavy metal base is ideal. As for gamepads, a number of manufacturers offer a variety of joystick configurations that range in price from a couple to hundreds of dollars. I've been a fan of high-end Thrustmaster products for years. The top-of-the-line Hotas Warthog and throttle package is made with solid plastic and metal construction and modeled against authentic joysticks used in real-world fighter jets (it's even officially licensed by the U.S. Air Force).[11] In addition to flight simulators, the Thrustmaster joystick-plus-throttle combination works great with big mech robot games. It's one of the most expensive PC gaming peripherals on the market, but for die-hard flight-simulation fanatics, it's the only controller that feels perfect.

10. http://www.microsoft.com/hardware/en-us/p/xbox-360-controller-for-windows
11. http://www.thrustmaster.com/en_US/products/hotas-warthog

Wrap-Up

In this chapter we connected several high-end peripherals, with the most important being the Corsair K95 keyboard and M95 mouse. We also powered up our awesome PC for the first time and felt the rush of adrenaline when we heard the fans spin up and saw the UEFI BIOS screen being displayed. We concluded by looking at peripherals designed to extend our computing experiences beyond the basic input of a standard keyboard, mouse, and monitor.

In the next chapter we will complete our journey by installing an operating system that will communicate with and drive all the hardware that we've assembled.

CHAPTER 7

Operating Systems

We have all the hardware in place for our PC to reach its high-end potential. But without an operating system to instruct all these pieces to talk to one another, we just have an organized collection of metals and plastics. This brief chapter will discuss the operating systems we can install that will bring to life the hardware we assembled.

Microsoft Windows

Microsoft Windows is the OS of choice among PC builders, and for good reason. Given Microsoft's dominance in the PC industry, it's the commercial standard by which PC-hardware manufacturers write drivers. All of the hardware recommended in this book "just works" with Windows. Most of the hardware will be automatically detected by Windows upon bootup, though some will need additional software drivers freely available for download from the respective hardware manufacturers' websites.

For example, the motherboard's optical audio output requires the Realtek audio drivers available from the ASUS website to get Windows to properly recognize and configure the hardware. Likewise, the Corsair K95 keyboard and M95 mouse will function on a basic level using the built-in drivers provided by Windows. But if you want to take advantage of the LED key lighting on the K95 or the flashing custom button settings on the M95, you will need to install the Windows drivers available from the Corsair website.

As for the version of Windows preferred, I recommend the 64-bit version of Windows 8.1. This latest release fixes a number of user-interface issues that were not fully realized in the initial release of Windows 8. Others might try to convince you to install the 32-bit version of Windows 7 instead. I advise against that for the simple reason that Microsoft and its hardware partners are moving forward with Windows 8. While Windows 7 will continue to be supported for at least a few years, Windows 8 is where the action is. And by installing the 64-bit release, you will be further future-proofing your hardware and software investments to run for years to come.

Installing Windows

Installing Microsoft Windows is as easy as inserting the Windows installation DVD-ROM into your PC's DVD or Blu-ray disc drive and rebooting your computer. Since no existing OS resides on the new SSD we installed, the Windows installation setup will launch from the DVD-ROM and walk you through the process of formatting and installing Windows on the SSD.

Microsoft has done a pretty good job with Windows 8.1 recognizing the various pieces of hardware installed on your computer. However, not everything is correctly detected or has the optimized drivers for the target hardware. In particular, the motherboard and graphics card are two critical pieces of hardware that need the drivers that came with them. You can install the drivers that came with the motherboard and graphics card CD-ROM, but it's best to download the latest drivers directly from the respective manufacturers' websites. For the Maximus VI Formula motherboard, install the various Windows 8.1 64-bit drivers and applications from the ASUS website.[1] Likewise, download the latest NVIDIA GeForce Experience application (which will automatically alert you to the latest driver updates for the GTX 780 Ti card) from the NVIDIA website.[2] The GeForce Experience application will also install the drivers for the 3D Vision 2 kit.

Once the up-to-date motherboard and graphics-card drivers are installed, visit the Corsair website for the K95 keyboard and M95 mouse firmware updates, configuration applications, and drivers.[3] If you also opted to install a peripheral like the Logitech G27 Racing Wheel, be sure to download and install the Logitech Gaming Software 64-bit package from the company's website as well.[4]

Now that all the hardware drivers are installed, it's time to update the UEFI BIOS on the motherboard. You can do this in several ways, but the easiest is to use ASUS's EZ Update Windows-based application that was installed along with the other motherboard drivers and utilities. EZ Update will automatically check ASUS's website for any BIOS updates. If there are any, the

---

1. http://www.asus.com/support/Download/1/45/MAXIMUS_VI_FORMULA/41/
2. http://www.geforce.com/geforce-experience
3. http://www.corsair.com/en-us/support/downloads
4. http://www.logitech.com/en-us/support/g27-racing-wheel?section=downloads

program will give you the option to download and install the update right from the Windows desktop. This is so much easier than the old way of storing the BIOS update files on a boot floppy, CD-ROM, or external USB drive, rebooting the computer, and hoping the update goes smoothly. Instead, EZ Update does all the work. Thanks to the application, manually keeping up to date on the latest UEFI BIOS versions is a thing of the past. Of course, if you prefer to update the BIOS the old-fashioned way, the UEFI BIOS used by the Maximus VI Formula motherboard allows you to do so.

That's all there is to it. You're ready to install the latest high-end games, video-editing software, sophisticated software-development tools, and whatever else you want your PC to run. But before we conclude this chapter, let's take a brief look at two alternative x86-based operating systems compatible with the hardware we assembled.

Ubuntu Linux

The various Linux distributions that run on desktop computers have come a long way since the '90s. The first time I ran Linux, I had to compile the kernel, graphics, and sound drivers myself. Every year since then has been "the year of the Linux desktop," with hopes that Linux would gain considerable traction in the desktop computing space. Linux has been far more successful in the mobile space in terms of sheer numbers (if you have an Android phone, you have a Linux-based computer), but the major Linux distributors are still attempting to improve the desktop experience to the level of commercial operating systems like Microsoft's Windows or Apple's Mac OS X.

Of all the Linux distributions available today, I consistently find the desktop edition of Ubuntu Linux to be of highest friendly compatibility with a majority of PC hardware.[5] Based on Debian Linux, Ubuntu is one of the most popular Linux distributions available. It's also free. Considering the amazing power that Ubuntu and other Linux distributions like Fedora, Mint, and Slackware deliver, it's stunning to realize that so much value is given away in the name of software freedom.

Ubuntu Linux can be installed side-by-side with existing OSs like Windows, or stand-alone. You can also run it inside a virtual machine using commercial solutions like VMware's Workstation or free alternatives like Oracle's VirtualBox.[6,7] If you have never used Linux before and already have Windows

---

5. http://www.ubuntu.com
6. http://www.vmware.com/products/workstation/
7. https://www.virtualbox.org

installed, I recommend using one of these virtual-machine containers to get an idea of what desktop Linux looks like and how it behaves.

Linux is very powerful but also not nearly as well supported as Windows, especially for custom peripherals. For example, while our K95 keyboard and M95 mouse will operate under Linux, we won't have the luxury of programmable keybindings or mouse-button assignments like we do in Windows. Other peripherals, such as NVIDIA's 3D Vision 2, are simply not supported under any operating system except Windows.

That said, I ran Linux as my primary desktop for a few years when games, video editing, and entertainment took a backseat to programming and system/network administration. But with the release of some amazing games and 3D Blu-ray titles, I made the switch back to Windows. I do miss the raw power, flexibility, and freedom that Linux has to offer, and I may make the switch again to Linux (or at least to a dual-boot system running Windows and Linux) with the release of Valve's SteamOS.

SteamOS

Valve Corporation, best known for its Half-Life and Portal games as well as its popular Steam software-distribution platform, has released its version of a Linux OS, SteamOS.[8] It was created partly in reaction to Microsoft's intent to compete with Valve and partly due to Valve's intention to not be beholden to the whims of an OS provider.

As I write this, SteamOS has not yet been released in final form, but you can download the beta and give it a try.[9] You can install it in either dedicated or dual-boot mode, and it should run quite well on the hardware we assembled in this book.

SteamOS, like Ubuntu, is a free OS that anyone with an x86-based computer can install and run. However, unlike Ubuntu, SteamOS is not designed to be a general-purpose operating system. Rather, it is optimized for games and other forms of digital-media entertainment.

Like Ubuntu, SteamOS is also a Debian Linux distribution derivative, but unlike Ubuntu, SteamOS is being optimized primarily for living-room entertainment. Given that, graphics and sound drivers are being tweaked to take advantage of high performance and throughput. There are great expectations that games may run even faster on SteamOS than on Windows running on

8.   http://store.steampowered.com/livingroom/SteamOS/
9.   http://store.steampowered.com/steamos/download?

the same hardware. This is because Valve can modify the source of the OS to suit its needs. Since SteamOS's intention is to act as a Steam client container for game playing, it doesn't need to make a general-purpose OS.

Ultimately, Valve is hoping to democratize the living-room gaming set-top box with SteamOS and compete against companies like Microsoft, Sony, and Nintendo. Rather than having a single company provide the hardware and entertainment-optimized OS, Valve is taking a page from Microsoft's playbook by providing the software reference platform to hardware manufacturers. Unlike Microsoft, though, Valve is giving the OS away for free and hoping that more devices running SteamOS will mean more customers using and buying software from the Steam distribution service. Dubbed Steamboxes, these set-top boxes running SteamOS are essentially variants of the type of computer we built in this book. As you can imagine, the cost of our PC is quite a bit more than a PS4 or Xbox One, which will continue to be a challenge for SteamOS's adoption.

In the meantime, SteamOS will be an interesting experiment that expands the role of Linux beyond the mobile and desktop space. If all you want to do is play games on your PC and are not interested in paying for a commercial operating system like Windows, SteamOS may be just what you're looking for.

Figure 74—This battle station is fully operational.

That's a Wrap!

Congratulations on building your PC. You've been on quite a journey and should be proud of what you have accomplished. You are now part of an elite group of people capable of building their own powerful personal computer to whatever specifications best suit their needs. And you can treat yourself to a nice reward using all the money you saved as a result.

Remember to share your experiences and even photos of your final build with other readers on the book's forum. I am really looking forward to seeing and reading about all the great work you have accomplished!

Beyond Awesome

As you acclimate to your new PC and discover just how powerful it is, you may begin wondering if there are ways to take it to even loftier performance heights. Let's look at some tips and suggestions for taking your PC hardware to the next level.

The key areas of improvement are in performance and presentation. We'll begin and end with a few suggestions for sprucing up your awesome PC to make it look as cool as it runs.

Cable Management

As the term implies, cable management is, quite simply, managing cables in an orderly and functional fashion. Keeping cables out of the way of components allows much easier access and servicing of those parts. Hard-core PC builders take great pride in the tight bundling and symmetric organization of cable layouts. Some even go as far as to install LEDs to accent the neatly routed cables and parts within a PC case. Such PC cases feature sides with clear plastic or plexiglass cutouts to view the layout within.

The amount of time and attention devoted to cable management is really a matter of personal preference. If you are the type of person who prefers working in a clean environment where even the paperclips are sorted by length, you will want to spend the extra effort to ensure cable runs are snug and well fitted. On the other hand, if you don't mind a messy workplace as long as it's functional, you will likely be satisfied with leaving the cables lay as they will as long as they do their job.

I decided not to spend much time on cable management during the initial build of the PC for a couple of reasons. Thanks to the cable design of the power supply we used, we didn't have a lot of excess power cables flopping about. Threading cables through the grommets also helped keep cables out of the way. If you look at the inside of the PC we built, there are barely any loose cables we need to worry about tying down. And since the case we're using to house our PC components doesn't have a plexiglass side to peer into the innards, it's not the end of the world if a few cables are not resting in perfect alignment with the shape of the case.

Perhaps the biggest reason for not zip-tieing everything down is because you will inevitably want to enhance your PC with additional expansion cards, cooling fans, and peripherals. When you do, you will likely need to reroute and restrap a portion of your cables anyway. Personally, I would hold off on any extensive cable-management effort until you're satisfied that you've built out your PC with everything you need, whether that's a full bay of SSDs and HDDs or tubing for water-cooling your PC.

Of course, if you can't live without knowing that a few wires are not pristinely tied down, then by all means take the time to align each cable. Check that the cables and wires collectively curve around each bend. Zip-tie them into place using the die-cut notches on the case to hold their shape and orientation (see the next figure).

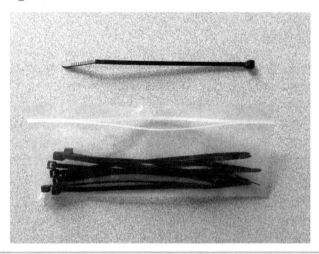

Figure 75—You can use the zip ties that accompanied the case to secure loose cables.

For inspiration from some truly impressive cabling schemes, check out the photos posted to the cable-management subreddit.[1]

---

1.   http://www.reddit.com/r/cablemanagement/

Overclocking

Earlier in the book, we touched on the idea of overclocking. Overclocking essentially pushes the running speed of the computer beyond the standard operating limits. While overclocking is most often applied to making the CPU run faster by increasing its clock frequency (from, say, 3.5 GHz to 4.2 GHz), other components, including the GPU on the graphics card, can be overclocked as well. The faster these chips run, the more data they can process in less time. The result is often manifested in faster boot times as well as faster and smoother video animations and transitions.

 Plan ahead and research the optimal settings to use when configuring overclocking values. Extreme overclocking can severely damage your hardware!

The stock settings for the motherboard are set for the greatest level of hardware compatibility and system stability. However, because we purchased a motherboard and graphics card specifically designed to be overclocked, we can take advantage of these parameters and tweak the settings accordingly.

ASUS makes overclocking a breeze with its Maximus VI Formula UEFI BIOS settings. When the PC turns on, press the F2 or Delete key to enter the UEFI settings screen. From there you can tweak a number of options—way too many to list here. The board allows access to so many options to tweak and overclock the frequencies of your hardware that you really need to know what you're doing before you start changing the default values. Otherwise your system may become unstable to the point of the operating system not even booting up. Fortunately, you can always reset these values to their recommended defaults should your computer start behaving erratically (stuttering mouse movements or sound, blocky messes appearing onscreen, random lock-ups, and so on).

The fastest way to take advantage of the optimal speed of the DDR3 2400 RAM we installed is to instruct the Ai Overclock Tuner in the BIOS to use XMP (Intel's Extreme Memory Profile) Profile #1, as shown in Figure 76, *Setting the XMP option to Profile #1 will noticeably improve your computer's performance*, on page 88. Doing so will boost the RAM frequencies to their optimal speeds. You can also tweak CPU settings such as cache ratios, PLL overvoltage, power phase, and current capability within the UEFI BIOS configuration.

As you become more familiar with your system's capabilities and limitations, you can manually modify a broad range of settings to home in on the perfect overclocked configuration for your system. Visit the hardware forums on the

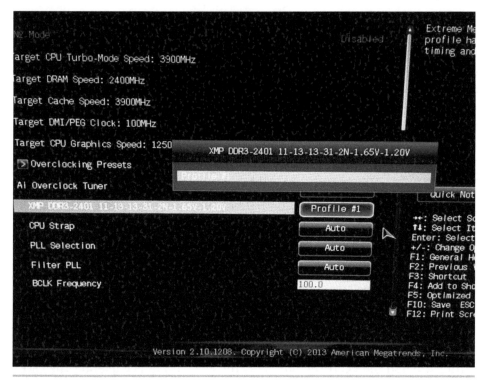

Figure 76—Setting the XMP option to Profile #1 will noticeably improve your computer's performance.

ASUS website to see what other Maximus VI users have successfully configured for their motherboard and PC setups.[2]

You can also use the ASUS AI Suite 3 utility designed for Windows operating systems. AI Suite 3 allows you to change various motherboard settings as well as upgrade the BIOS straight from the Windows desktop. It's a nice convenience to have and makes tweaking easier because you can change various settings on your motherboard while following along with references in a web browser in a separate window, as shown in Figure 77, *The AI Suite 3 application allows you to monitor and modify motherboard settings in real time*, on page 89.

RAID

RAID stands for redundant array of independent disks, and as the name implies, it's a technology that combines a number of physically separate hard

---

2. http://rog.asus.com/forum/forumdisplay.php?39-General-Hardware-Overclocking-amp-Tweaking

Figure 77—The AI Suite 3 application allows you to monitor and modify motherboard settings in real time.

drives to improve drive performance and/or reliability. Depending on how the RAID is configured, you can use it to double your file-storage throughput (great for large video-file editing), or rely on a failover drive to keep the system running in the event of the primary drive dying. You can also combine these configurations for the best of both worlds, assuming you have the money and enough drive bays to house the extra hardware.

Many types of RAID configurations exist. You can research the different kinds on various websites, including Wikipedia,[3] but I'll cover the most popular here.

RAID 0 is used to attain the fastest data read-write speeds possible. For example, in a two-drive RAID 0 setup, the data is striped across both drives. Doing so effectively doubles the read-write performance. The major disadvantage to RAID 0 is that if even one drive fails, you lose all the data on both drives.

3.   http://en.wikipedia.org/wiki/RAID

RAID 1 provides double the reliability at half the capacity. In a two-drive RAID 1 configuration, if one drive fails, your data is safely mirrored on the other working drive.

RAID 5 offers better performance, greater storage capacity, and better reliability than RAID 1. It requires a minimum of three drives. RAID 5 configurations are mostly for business use, with an emphasis on database transaction processing.

RAID 10 combines the speed of RAID 0 and the reliability of RAID 1. RAID 10 requires a minimum of four drives, with two drives striped for RAID 0–level speed and the other two drives mirroring the striped drives for reliability. RAID 10 configurations are expensive due to the number of disks required and are somewhat complex to correctly set up.

To set up any of the RAID configurations I've mentioned, enter the Maximus VI UEFI BIOS screen for RAID settings in the Advanced -> SATA Configuration screen. Set the SATA mode to the RAID mode you want to create, save the changes, and reboot. Then enter the Intel Rapid Storage Technology Option ROM utility during bootup by pressing Ctrl-I. Follow the screen menus to create a RAID set, identifying which drives will be part of the RAID and what RAID level they should be set to. But be aware that any time you create or remove a RAID configuration, you will lose all data on the target drives.

RAID Is Not the Same as a Backup

RAID configurations are not replacements for file backups. Even though a properly configured RAID can help protect against drive failure, you should still back up important data files to secure off-site storage. Using third-party cloud-based service providers is fine for small files, but if you have a large catalog of media files, it's best to purchase an external drive that can be used for regular backups. When you're done backing up to the external drive, store the drive off-site at a trusted family member's or friend's home for extra safety.

Keep in mind that even with a regular backup in place, restoring a full drive containing multiple terabytes could take hours or even days. But at least you will have the data intact should your primary storage hardware fail!

Water Cooling

Compared to the traditional air-cooling approach we used in this book, water cooling offers a more effective and possibly less noisy approach to reducing heat buildup in your awesome PC. The concept behind water cooling is straightforward, taking its inspiration from a car radiator. An electric pump circulates cool water (or another heat-dissipating liquid) that flows through tubing connected to areas of heat buildup. These are most often the CPU and GPU. As the cooled liquid passes over these hot parts, the heat is transferred by convection and carried away as the water recirculates over a radiator. While fanless radiators exist, the most common water-cooled systems have radiators with usually two or more fans to help cool the heated liquid as it passes through the metal fins of the radiator.

When assembling the parts for this book, I initially considered using a Corsair H100i water-cooled CPU fan in lieu of the Cooler Master Hyper N520. But I opted for the more traditional air-cooled approach for three important reasons: cost, efficacy, and safety.

Unless you intend to perform some really heat-searing CPU overclocking, the Cooler Master Hyper N520 should perform admirably at keeping your CPU well within safe operating temperature ranges. A water-cooled CPU component that accomplishes the same objective costs nearly $100 more. And while it's rare (especially with parts that are self-contained like Corsair's Hydro Series liquid CPU cooler), leaks can and do occur. A major leak can become a safety hazard and quickly render your expensive computer useless.

But the good news is that the parts I chose for the PC can easily be upgraded with water-cooled components whenever you're ready to do so. Everything from the case to the motherboard is water-cool-ready, with the only added cost being the expense of the additional pump, radiator, fans, clamps, and tubing needed to upgrade your PC to the next level of performance.

Bling

Did you try toggling on and off the front and side fan LEDs of the 500R PC case? Pressing the fan's light button on the front panel of the PC case will turn on the white LEDs on the front- and side-panel fans, as shown in Figure 78, *The two front-panel case fans with LEDs turned on*, on page 92. Even though these lights add no computational value to the PC, they elevate spinning plastic and metal to a mood-inducing level of cool.

PC lighting has become an art form in and of itself, further defining the individualized nature of the personal computer. As you continue to enhance and improve your computer with hardware upgrades, you can highlight these components with recessed LED strips that backlight the operating gear. If the default blue lights are too subdued for your tastes, you can swap out the chassis fans with different-colored replacements.

Figure 78—The two front-panel case fans with LEDs turned on

Even graphics cards like the GTX 780 Ti that we installed have unique lighting schemes. For example, the GeForce logo along the top of the card can fade on and off, blink, and even pulsate in time with audio playback. You can access these settings via NVIDIA's GeForce Experience LED Visualizer,[4] as shown in Figure 79, *The GeForce logo lighting style on the top of the GTX 780 Ti card can be modified via the LED Visualizer dialog*, on page 93.

Naturally, to showcase the lighting schemes inside the case, you need to either replace the case sides with see-through plastic or entirely replace the case with a model that intentionally showcases the interior hardware. But now that you know how to assemble a personal computer from start to finish, transplanting your hardware from one case to another should be a stress-free procedure.

In addition to lighting, there's the option to deck out the fans, wires, and tubes with different color schemes. Fan blades and rings can be obtained in a variety of colors, along with matching LED backlighting. Enhancing your PC with such colorful additions can really set it apart and further define its operating intentions to match the personality of its owner. Have fun personalizing your awesome PC!

---

4. http://www.geforce.com/geforce-experience

Figure 79—The GeForce logo lighting style on the top of the GTX 780 Ti card can be modified via the LED Visualizer dialog.

The Complete Parts List

Here is the complete list of parts used to build the awesome PC featured in this book. You can comparison-shop for these items on popular e-commerce websites like Amazon, Micro Center, Newegg, and many others. Also follow the buildapcsales subreddit on Reddit or track the best prices on PC Part Picker to be alerted to the latest sales on these items.[1,2] In the following table, the Price column represents the best sale price listed on PC Part Picker at the time this list was compiled.

Packag-ing	Category	Description	Price
	Case	Corsair Carbide Series 500R mid tower	$79.99
	Power supply	Corsair RM850 850-watt ATX12V	$139.98
	CPU	Intel Core i7-4770K 3.5 GHz socket LGA 1150	$279.99
	Motherboard	ASUS Maximus VI Formula LGA 1150	$295.99
	CPU fan	Cooler Master Hyper N520	$38.98
	Thermal paste	Arctic Silver 5 high-density polysynthetic	$7.99

---

1. http://www.reddit.com/r/buildapcsales
2. http://pcpartpicker.com

Packag-ing	Category	Description	Price
	SDRAM	Corsair Vengeance Pro 16 GB 240-pin DDR3 2400	$199.99
	SSD	Samsung 840 Pro Series 256 GB SATA	$198.99
	HDD	Seagate 4 TB SATA 64 MB cache internal drive	$161.87
	DVD-ROM	ASUS DVD-ROM OEM drive	$19.99
	Blu-ray drive	LG WH14NS40 Blu-ray drive	$67.99
	Graphics card	ASUS GTX780TI-3GD5 GeForce GTX 780 Ti 3 GB GDDR5	$699.99
	Display	BenQ XL2720T 27" HDMI widescreen LCD monitor	$408.98
	Speakers	Logitech Speaker System Z906 (surround sound)	$326.66
	Headset	Corsair Vengeance 1500 Dolby 7.1 USB headset	$71.99
	Keyboard	Corsair Vengeance K95 mechanical keyboard	$147.98
	Mouse	Corsair Vengeance M95 Performance MMO/RTS laser mouse	$59.99
	Mouse mat	Corsair Vengeance MM200 Gaming Mouse Mat – Extended Edition	$32.99
	3D vision	NVIDIA 3D Vision 2 Wireless Glasses Kit	$149.99

Packaging	Category	Description	Price
	Game controller	Xbox 360 Wired Controller for Windows	$49.99
	Racing wheel	Logitech G27 Racing Wheel	$229.99
	OS	Windows 8.1 Pro System Builder OEM 64-bit	$137.97

With the exception of RAM, the prices listed in the table will most likely be lower by the time you read this. And there will also likely be new models available (particularly in motherboards and video cards). Such is the fast pace of change in the PC-hardware world. But the cool thing is you no longer need to worry about instant obsolescence. The PC built with these parts will remain on the cutting edge through 2015. And when a better graphics card or faster SSDs come along, you can easily swap out and sell your existing hardware to keep your home-built PC on the leading performance edge for years to come.

Additional Resources

Besides the go-to-first Google and YouTube searches, here is a list of helpful websites to further enhance your PC-building expertise:

- Choose My PC quickly generates simple PC build configurations based on power-versus-price variables. Useful for estimating build expenses.[1]

- PC Part Picker is an excellent price-monitoring website that can be used to compare the historical and current sale prices of a variety of PC components among popular e-commerce websites.[2]

- PC-related subgroups on Reddit, such as buildapc and buildapcsales, host useful forums to stay up to date on the latest trends, discussions, and sales-related notices about PC hardware.[3,4]

- Tom's Hardware offers in-depth analysis and reviews of most of today's cutting-edge PC hardware.[5]

1. http://www.choosemypc.net
2. http://pcpartpicker.com
3. http://www.reddit.com/r/buildapc/
4. http://www.reddit.com/r/buildapcsales/
5. http://www.tomshardware.com

More Books by Mike Riley

Program your home automation with Arduino's and Android, and Script your Android device right on the device itself!

Programming Your Home

Take control of your home! Programmatically interact with indoor and outdoor lighting, remotely monitor and take charge of your home's security, react to changes in room lighting and temperature by autonomously opening and closing curtains, and much more. Learn how to program Android smartphones and Arduino microcontrollers to remotely manage your home's environment. Step-by-step instructions tell you all you need to know about how to obtain, build, program, use, and extend these innovative services.

Mike Riley
(242 pages) ISBN: 9781934356906. $33
http://pragprog.com/book/mrhome

Developing Android on Android

Take advantage of the open, tinker-friendly Android platform and make your device work the way you want it to. Quickly create Android tasks, scripts, and programs entirely on your Android device—no PC required. Learn how to build your own innovative Android programs and workflows with tools you can run on Android itself, and tailor the Android default user interface to match your mobile lifestyle needs. Apply your favorite scripting language to rapidly develop programs that speak the time and battery level, alert you to important events or locations, read your new email to you, and much more.

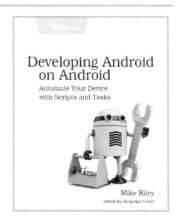

Mike Riley
(232 pages) ISBN: 9781937785543. $15
http://pragprog.com/book/mrand

The Pragmatic Bookshelf

The Pragmatic Bookshelf features books written by developers for developers. The titles continue the well-known Pragmatic Programmer style and continue to garner awards and rave reviews. As development gets more and more difficult, the Pragmatic Programmers will be there with more titles and products to help you stay on top of your game.

Visit Us Online

This Book's Home Page
http://pragprog.com/book/mrpc
Source code from this book, errata, and other resources. Come give us feedback, too!

Register for Updates
http://pragprog.com/updates
Be notified when updates and new books become available.

Join the Community
http://pragprog.com/community
Read our weblogs, join our online discussions, participate in our mailing list, interact with our wiki, and benefit from the experience of other Pragmatic Programmers.

New and Noteworthy
http://pragprog.com/news
Check out the latest pragmatic developments, new titles and other offerings.

Save on the eBook

Save on the eBook versions of this title. Owning the paper version of this book entitles you to purchase the electronic versions at a terrific discount.

PDFs are great for carrying around on your laptop—they are hyperlinked, have color, and are fully searchable. Most titles are also available for the iPhone and iPod touch, Amazon Kindle, and other popular e-book readers.

Buy now at *http://pragprog.com/coupon*

Contact Us

Online Orders:	*http://pragprog.com/catalog*
Customer Service:	*support@pragprog.com*
International Rights:	*translations@pragprog.com*
Academic Use:	*academic@pragprog.com*
Write for Us:	*http://pragprog.com/write-for-us*
Or Call:	+1 800-699-7764

Milton Keynes UK
Ingram Content Group UK Ltd.
UKHW050854121223
434194UK00005B/40